NEWSPAPER LIBRARIES:
A BIBLIOGRAPHY, 1933-1985

NEWSPAPER LIBRARIES:
A BIBLIOGRAPHY, 1933-1985

Compiled by
Celia Jo Wall

Harry Lee Waterfield Library
Murray State University

1986
Special Libraries Association Washington, D.C.

Copyright © 1986 by Special Libraries Association
1700 Eighteenth Street, N.W., Washington, D.C. 20009

Manufactured in the United States of America
All rights reserved

ISBN 0-87111-319-8

Library of Congress Cataloging-in-Publication Data
Wall, Celia.
   Newspaper libraries.

   Includes indexes.
   1. Newspaper and periodical libraries—
Bibliography. I. Title.
Z675.N37W34   1986   016.026'07   86-14604
ISBN 0-87111-319-8

Dedicated to WCM, my best friend.

TABLE OF CONTENTS

Introduction 1

General References
    (Items 1-138) 4

The History of Newspaper Libraries
    (Items 139-238) .18

Organization and Administration of Newspaper Libraries
    (Items 239-288) .27

Classification and Filing
    (Items 289-389) .32

Reference Materials in the Newspaper Library
    (Items 390-401) .43

Newspaper Indexing
    (Items 402-521) .45

Microforms
    (Items 522-563) .57

Automation and the Newspaper Library
    (Items 564-782) .62

Newspaper Librarianship
    (Items 783-805) .85

Appendixes 88

Author Index 96

Subject Index. 114

INTRODUCTION

The last decade has been a period of tremendous change in the newspaper industry. Computers have invaded nearly every department of the average newspaper. From the composing room to the circulation department, the new technology is evident. Newspaper accounting offices have microfiche readers on employees' desks so that personnel and bookkeeping records on COM can be quickly accessed. Composing room linotype machines have been replaced by phototypesetters. VDT's sit where typewriters once did in newsrooms. In recent years, computers have even found their way into the last stronghold of manual tedium -- the newspaper library.

The last half of the 1970's saw reports of newspapers such as the Boston Globe, The (Louisville, KY) Courier-Journal, and others exploring ways in which computers could be used in their libraries to improve the accuracy and speed with which information was stored and retrieved. In the 1980's, full-text storage and retrieval of news articles is a working reality. The newspaper library of the 1980's is a far cry from the "morgue" of yesterday which many times only contained biographical material to be used in preparing obituaries. The computer has brought the promise of a new, exciting, and challenging future to the newspaper library.

However, the computer has not solved all of the newspaper library's problems. For every problem solved, it seems new ones have been created and some existing ones magnified. A poor manual system in a newspaper library cannot simply be transferred to a computer and thereby improved. Problems with the manual system must first be recognized and addressed before the computer is introduced. If reporters cannot locate clippings in the files because there is no up-to-date subject authority list to guide them, converting to a computer system will only make the need for such an authority list more evident and urgent. So while newspaper libraries are now headed in a new direction, it is still vital that people dealing with them be aware of the background of the libraries and their problems. Problems which now exist and must be solved were created in the past. Perhaps understanding where the problems came from and why they exist will make solving them easier. This bibliography has been compiled to make research on newspaper libraries easier.

THE LITERATURE OF NEWSPAPER LIBRARIES

At the end of Geoffrey Whatmore's book News Information: The Organization of Press Cuttings in the Libraries of Newspaper and Broadcasting Services (1964), the author included a "Bibliographical Note" which begins, "The book has no bibliography because there has been little written on the subject of newspaper libraries." He then went on to list the four books and pamphlets which did exist: *Newspaper Reference Methods* (1933) by Robert W. Desmond; *Newspaper Indexing* (1942) by H.W. Friedman; *Newspaper Libraries* (1952) by J. Lewis; and *The Newspaper Reference Library* (1950) published by Colenso Press.

Ten years later, Whatmore wrote a similar note at the end of the article on "News Libraries and Collections" which he wrote for the *Encyclopedia of Library and Information Science* (1976). At the beginning of the article's bibliography Whatmore wrote, "The literature of news libraries is not extensive." He then proceeded to list the same four books as he had in 1964 with two additions: his own *News Information* (1964) and *Guidelines for Newspaper Libraries* (1975) which had been published by the American Newspaper Publishers Association. These titles he supplemented with material from periodical literature.

The literature on newspaper libraries is not extensive compared to other areas, but for the researcher who is willing to do some digging there is enough to make the search worthwhile. The six books and pamphlets listed by Whatmore in 1976 still serve as the major book sources on newspaper libraries. This can easily be supplemented by periodical articles, many of which appear in *Special Libraries*. The introduction of the computer into newspaper libraries has added some new sources of information, e.g. the *Journal of Library Automation*, and publications of the American Society of Information Science discuss automation practices in newspaper libraries. In addition, the newspaper industry provides sources for those within the industry which are often not indexed or publicized outside the field. For instance, the library of the American Newspaper Publishers Association (ANPA) is an excellent source of information and material on newspaper libraries, as is the Newspaper Division of the Special Libraries Association. (See Appendix for additional information.)

Two problems exist for the average researcher trying to access the literature of newspaper libraries. First, many articles written on these libraries are of little or no use to the serious researcher. Second, much of the literature is not indexed in the standard periodical indexes. *Library Literature* indexes *Special Libraries*, but where does a researcher go to see if trade journals such as *Presstime*, *Newspaper Controller*, and others have carried articles on newspaper libraries? It is hoped that this bibliography will help to solve, or at least lessen, these two problems.

SCOPE OF THE BIBLIOGRAPHY

The purpose of this bibliography is to try to provide as complete a list as possible of English-language material written on newspaper libraries from 1933 through 1985. Citations include books, parts of books, professional and trade journal articles, technical memorandums, and pamphlets. In addition, an attempt has been made to locate and include unpublished material which, in this particular field, may actually be of greater practical value than some of the published material. Examples of such materials are college and university theses and the transcripts of speeches presented at meetings of the Newspaper Division of SLA. Copies of these transcripts are frequently available from the American Newspaper Publishers Association (ANPA). Such availability is indicated in the bibliography by an ANPA number in parenthesis following an entry, e.g. (ANPA 67-2).

Anyone interested in the literature of newspaper libraries before 1933 is referred to Desmond's <u>Newspaper Reference Methods</u>. This classic work was published by The University of Minnesota Press in 1933 and includes a comprehensive bibliography of articles up to that time.

LIMITATIONS OF THE BIBLIOGRAPHY

The user of this bibliography should keep three things in mind:

-- First, this is not a selective bibliography listing only the most "relevant" sources. The quality and usefulness of the material cited varies greatly.

-- Second, this work includes only that material which deals specifically with newspaper libraries. For example, an article on newspaper indexing will be included; an article on the general principles of indexing will not.

-- Third, citations are not included for the newsletter of the Newspaper Division of SLA since this publication has its own indexes. (See Appendix for further information on the Newspaper Division and its publications.)

GENERAL REFERENCES

1. "ANPA Survey of Newspaper Libraries - How They Operate and Look to Future." *Special Libraries* 57 (November 1966): 654-657.

2. Albert, W.J. "The Morgue Isn't a Morgue Anymore." Paper presented at the 57th Annual Conference of the Special Libraries Association, Minneapolis, MN, May 29-June 2 1966. (ANPA 66-1)

3. Alcott, William. "Newspaper Library and the Army, Navy and FBI." *Special Libraries* 34 (July-August 1943): 308-310, 346. Paper presented before the Newspaper Group at the 35th Annual Conference of the Special Libraries Association, New York, NY, 21-25 June 1943.

4. Alcott, William. "Report of the Editor of the Newspaper Manual; Abridged." *Special Libraries* 31 (July-August 1940): 240-241.

5. Altschull, Herbert. Review of *Directory of Newspaper Libraries in United States and Canada*, edited by Grace D. Parch. *American Historical Review* 82 (1977): 1068-1069.

6. Anderson, Elizabeth L., ed. *Newspaper Libraries in the U.S. and Canada*. New York: Special Libraries Association, 1980.

7. Arany, Lawrence A. "Serving Two Masters With One Library." Paper presented at the 57th Annual Conference of the Special Libraries Association, Minneapolis, MN, May 29-June 2 1966. (ANPA 66-2)

8. "Archivist Keeps Tabs on History of *L.A. Times*." *Editor and Publisher* 111 (April 22, 1978): 35.

9. "Are Newspaper Rooms Necessary?" *New Zealand Libraries* 6 (May 1943): 147-148.

10. Austin, Neal F. "The Newspaper Library: The Results of a Survey Completed in June 1949." <u>Special Libraries</u> 41 (February 1950): 42-46.

11. Barger, Floyd. "The Changing Newspaper." Paper presented at the 58th Annual Conference of the Special Libraries Association, New York, NY, May 28-June 1 1967. (ANPA 67-2)

12. Bertleson, Arthur. "Don't Keep Your Imagination in the Morgue." Paper presented at the 55th Annual Conference of the Special Libraries Association, St. Louis, MO, 7-11 June 1964. (ANPA 64-1)

13. Burness, Jack; Clement G. Vitek; and Milton Prensky. "Proposed Standards for Newspaper Libraries." <u>Special Libraries</u> 51 (November 1960): 501-504. Paper presented at the 51st Annual Conference of the Special Libraries Association, Cleveland, OH, 5-8 June 1960.

14. Carrick, Kathleen. "Informing the Media." Paper presented at the 66th Annual Conference of the Special Libraries Association, Chicago, IL, 8-12 June 1975. (ANPA 75-2)

15. Chase, William D. "A Newspaper Librarian Looks at the Calendar." Paper presented at the 55th Annual Conference of the Special Libraries Association, St. Louis, MO, 7-11 June 1964. (ANPA 64-2)

16. Cohen, Diana M. "Content Analysis of Information about Newspapers and News Magazine Libraries in Selected Literature of Journalism, 1967-71." Research Paper, Kent State University, 1973.

17. Cohen, Madeline. "ABC News Information Center." Paper presented at the 75th Annual Conference of the Special Libraries Association, New York, NY, 9-14 June 1984. (ANPA 84-2)

18. Conklin, Florina. "Building a Newspaper Library." Paper presented at the 54th Annual Conference of the Special Libraries Association, Denver, CO, 9-13 June 1963. (ANPA 63-3)

19. Daniel, Clifton. "Newspapers, Librarians and History." Paper presented at the 58th Annual Conference of the Special Libraries Association, New York, NY, May 28-June 1 1967. (ANPA 67-3)

20. De'Ath, David. "A Survey of Newspaper Libraries and Their Problems." Master's thesis, City University (London), Centre for Information Science, 1977.

21. Desmond, Robert W. Newspaper Reference Methods. Minneapolis, MN: The University of Minnesota Press, 1933.

22. Dezanni, David. "Herbert vs. Lando." Paper presented at the 70th Annual Conference of the Special Libraries Association, Honolulu, HI, 9-14 June 1979. (ANPA 79-2)

23. DuBois, Beatrice. "The ANPA Library and Newspaper Information Service." Paper presented at the 54th Annual Conference of the Special Libraries Association, Denver, CO, 9-13 June 1963. (ANPA 63-4)

24. Eads, Roscoe C. "Do You Run a Library, Reference Room or a Morgue?" Paper presented at the 55th Annual Conference of the Special Libraries Association, St. Louis, MO, 7-11 June 1964. (ANPA 64-3)

25. Eads, Roscoe C. "New Library System; History in Clippings." Editor and Publisher 100 (February 25, 1967): 56.

26. Eads, Roscoe C. "Purpose of Library Survey." Paper presented at the 54th Annual Conference of the Special Libraries Association, Denver, CO, 9-13 June 1963. (ANPA 63-5)

27. Eads, Roscoe C. "The Responsibilities of the Newspaper Library to Future Historians." Special Libraries 55 (January 1964): 26-28. Paper presented at the 54th Annual Conference of the Special Libraries Association, Denver, CO, 9-13 June 1963.

28. "Editor Urges Library Help for Reporters." Editor and Publisher 102 (June 14, 1969): 32.

29. Ellis, Edgar. "Information Please; Abridged." Special Libraries 31 (July-August 1940): 237. Paper presented at the 32nd Annual Conference of the Special Libraries Association, Indianapolis, IN, 3-6 June 1940.

30. Elston, Wilbur. "Confessions of a Friend of the Library." Paper presented at the 61st Annual Conference of the Special Libraries Association, Detroit, MI, 7-11 June 1970. (ANPA 70-2)

31. Fenimore, Jean H. "What's Wrong with Newspaper Libraries?" Special Libraries 36 (April 1945): 111-113.

32. "40 Librarians Have Workshop Over a Weekend." Editor and Publisher 105 (March 18, 1972): 20.

33. Garthwaite, Joan. "The Small Newspaper Library." New Jersey Libraries 2 (Spring 1969): 18-19.

34. Ginn, John C. "Financial Considerations: Staying in Touch with Reality." Paper presented at the 72nd Annual Conference of the Special Libraries Association, Atlanta, GA, 13-18 June 1981. (ANPA 81-4)

35. Grayland, Eugene Charles. The Newspaper Reference Library and the Filing and Uses of Press Clippings. 2nd edition. Auckland, New Zealand: Colenso Press, 1950.

36. Greene, Stephen A. "Who's Who in the Armed Services." Special Libraries 36 (April 1945): 120-123.

37. Griffin, John: J.S. Sossai; and Jim Richstad. "Impact on Information Availability in Asia and Its Two-Way Flow." Paper presented at the 70th Annual Conference of the Special Libraries Association, Honolulu, HI, 9-14 June 1979. (ANPA 79-3)

38. Guidelines for Newspaper Libraries. Reston, VA: American Newspaper Publishers Association Foundation, 1974, 1976, 1983. (For review article see entry for David M. Hoffman.)

39. Gupte, Pranay. "Who, What, When, Where and How Girls." *Editor and Publisher* 104 (April 3, 1971): 17.

40. Guzda, M.K. "Tips on Getting Your Newspaper's Library in Order." *Editor and Publisher* 117 (September 8, 1984): 20.

41. Hall, George. "An Editor Looks at the Newspaper Library." Paper presented at the 55th Annual Conference of the Special Libraries Association, St. Louis, MO, 7-11 June 1964. (ANPA 64-5)

42. Halloran, Vera. "Bureau of Advertising and the Newspaper Library." Paper presented at the 56th Annual Conference of the Special Libraries Association, Philadelphia, PA, 6-10 June 1965. (ANPA 65-5)

43. Harr, Luther A. "Newspaper Libraries - An Appreciation." *Special Libraries* 30 (November 1939): 298-300.

44. Harris, Jeanette F. "The Newspaper Library: Its History, Function, and Value with Special Reference to the *New York Herald Tribune*." Master's thesis, Southern Connecticut State College, October 1959.

45. "Hearst Gives Library to Texas University." *Editor and Publisher* 101 (May 25, 1968): 14.

46. Henebry, Agnes C. "How To's for the Small Newspaper Library." Paper presented at the 52nd Annual Conference of the Special Libraries Association, San Francisco, CA, May 28-June 1 1961. (ANPA 61-2)

47. Henebry, Agnes C. "Newspaper Library in a Small Newspaper Office." Washington, D.C.: American Newspaper Publishers Association, 1956.

48. Henebry, Agnes C. "The Smaller Newspaper Library." Paper presented at the 55th Annual Conference of the Special Libraries Association, St. Louis, MO, 7-11 June 1964. (ANPA 64-6)

49. Hine, Gladys. "Lessons for Leadership." Paper presented at the 55th Annual Conference of the Special Libraries Association, St. Louis, MO, 7-11 June 1964. (ANPA 64-7)

50. Hobby, Diana. "National Library Week in Texas: The Newspaper Library." *Texas Library Journal* 49 (May 1973): 61-62, 98.

51. Hoffman, David M. Review of *Guidelines for Newspaper Libraries*. *Library Journal* 108 (December 15, 1983): 2314.

52. Hunt, Mary Alice. "Survey of Florida Newspaper Libraries." Master's thesis, Florida State University, 1953.

53. Huskinson, A.H. "Newspaper Reference Libraries." *Librarian and Book World* 36 (April 1947): 65-67.

54. "Insurance for Newspaper Libraries." *Special Libraries* 57 (February 1966): 115-116.

55. Jacobus, Alma. "Binding in a Newspaper Library; Abridged." *Special Libraries* 31 (July-August 1940): 295.

56. Jennings, Anne B. "Regional Workshop on News Libraries." Paper presented at the 63rd Annual Conference of the Special Libraries Association, Boston, MA, 4-8 June 1972. (ANPA 72-2)

57. Jessup, Lee Cheney. "Newspaper Library." *Tennessee Librarian* 4 (May 1952): 6-8.

58. Johnson, DeWayne B. "Is Yours a Library or a Morgue?" *Quill* 57 (August 1969): 18.

59. Jones, Nancy C. "'Morgue' Is Dead: Well-Run Libraries Assist Reporters." *Editor and Publisher* 93 (January 16, 1960): 56-57.

60. Jones, Robert W. "The Editorial Writer and the Library." *Special Libraries* 21 (December 1940): 376-377.

61. Kremer, Valerie. "Newspaper Libraries Meet Daily Deadlines." *Feliciter* 22 (May 1976): 3.

62. Lewis, Chester Milton. "What's Your Information Rating?" *Special Libraries* 42 (September 1951): 249-254, 269-270. Paper presented before a joint meeting of the Newspaper and Publishing Divisions at the 42nd Annual Conference of the Special Libraries Association, St. Paul, MN, 18-21 June 1951.

63. Lewis, Joseph. *Newspaper Libraries*. Pamphlet No. 11. London: The Library Association, 1952.

64. Lutz, Doug. "Broadcast News Media Libraries, WNET/Thirteen." Paper presented at the 75th Annual Conference of the Special Libraries Association, New York, NY, 9-14 June 1984. (ANPA 84-5)

65. McCardle, L. "What Newspaper Librarians in the West are Doing." *Special Libraries Association Proceedings* 2 (1939): 100-102. Paper presented at the 31st Annual Conference of the Special Libraries Association, Baltimore, MD, 23-27 May 1939.

66. McGraw, Mary Drue. "Newspaper Libraries." *Florida Libraries* 10 (December 1959): 7-8+.

67. Mehta, D.S. "Newspaper Libraries." Master's thesis, Western Reserve University, School of Library Science, June 1955.

68. Miller, Diane. "Morgue Is Not Dead." *Illinois Libraries* 62 (March 1980): 250-252.

69. Mohr, Euruce Collins. "Cooperation Between Newspaper Libraries and School of Journalism Libraries." *Special Libraries* 38 (September 1947): 216-218. Paper presented at the 38th Annual Conference of the Newspaper Group of the Special Libraries Association, Chicago, IL, 10-13 June 1947.

70. Mooney, Shirley. "Newspaper Libraries." Paper presented at the 70th Annual Conference of the Special Libraries Association, Honolulu, HI, 9-14 June 1979. (ANPA 79-5)

71. Ndau, H.W. "Organising a Newspaper Cuttings Collection: One Way Out of the Maze for Small Libraries." MALA Bulletin 3 (July 1982): 22-25.

72. "Newark Gets News Files." New Jersey Libraries 6 (June 1973): 14.

73. "News Library Chiefs at API." Editor and Publisher 104 (May 8, 1971): 25.

74. "A Newspaper Library." Oklahoma Librarian 6 (September 1937): 3.

75. "Newspaper Reference Libraries." In The Reference Librarian in University, Municipal and Specialised Libraries, edited by James D. Stewart, 231-243. London: Grafton & Co., 1951.

76. Noyes, Linwood I. "ANPA: More Books Are Sought for Library." Editor and Publisher 92 (April 25, 1959): 78.

77. Orgain, Marian M. "Goals and Aims of Newspaper Libraries and Librarians." In Special Librarianship: A New Reader, 1980, edited by Eugene B. Jackson, 350-353. Metuchen, NJ: Scarecrow Press, 1980.

78. Palmer, E. Clephan. "The Library of a Daily Newspaper." Association of Special Libraries and Information Bureaux, London. Report of Proceedings of the Conference, 2 (1925): 136-137.

79. Parch, Grace D., ed. Directory of Newspaper Libraries in the United States and Canada. New York: Special Libraries Association, 1976. (For review article see entry for Herbert Altschull.)

80. Peterson, Agnes J. "Move Toward Research in the Newspaper Library." Special Libraries 29 (March 1938): 84-86.

81. Pettit, Ford M. "In Defense of Newspaper Libraries." Special Libraries 36 (April 1945): 113-116.

82. "Program to Raise Status of Library." *Editor and Publisher* 93 (July 9, 1960): 64.

83. Rouse, J. Michael. "One Editor's Advice to Librarians." Paper presented at the 74th Annual Conference of the Special Libraries Association, New Orleans, LA, 4-9 June 1983. (ANPA 83-3)

84. Samyasam Mukhopadhyay. "Press-Clipping Library." *Herald of Library Science* 23 (January - April 1984): 51-56.

85. Schaeffer, Rex. "How to Use Your Newspaper Library." Paper presented at the 57th Annual Conference of the Special Libraries Association, Minneapolis, MN, May 28 - June 1966. (ANPA 66-8)

86. Schaeffer, Rex. "What's New in Newspaper Libraries?" Paper presented at the 53rd Annual Conference of the Special Libraries Association, Washington, DC, 27-31 May 1962. (ANPA 62-6)

87. Schmidt, Richard; Inger Hansen; Dick Zweifel; and Michael Dagg. "Freedom of Information and the Information Specialist." Program presented at the 76th Annual Conference of the Special Libraries Association, Winnipeg, Canada, 8-13 June 1985.

88. Scofield, James S. *Information Services*. Arlington, VA: ERIC Document Reproduction Service, ED 107 277, 1973. Paper presented at the 64th Annual Conference of the Special Libraries Association, Pittsburgh, PA, 10-14 June 1973. (ANPA 73-7)

89. Scofield, James S. "The Mission of Newspaper Libraries." *Editor and Publisher* 117 (February 18, 1984): 52, 41.

90. Scofield, James S. "The Newspaper Library - Its Goal." Paper presented at the 67th Annual Conference of the Special Libraries Association, Denver, CO, 6-10 June 1976. (ANPA 76-11)

91. Scofield, James S. "Social Error." (letter) *Editor and Publisher* 100 (October 14, 1967): 7.

92. "Seminar Held on Upgrading News Libraries." *Editor and Publisher* 116 (June 18, 1984): 40.

93. Semonche, Barbara P. "Newspaper Libraries: History, Mystery and Info to Go." *Editor and Publisher* 117 (March 31, 1984): 48, 38, 33.

94. Semonche, Barbara P., ed. *Newspaper Libraries in North Carolina: 1981-1982 Illustrated Directory*. Durham, NC: Durham Herald Company, 1982.

95. Shaftesley, John M. "Newspaper Libraries." (letter) *The Indexer* 9 (October 1974): 57-58.

96. Sharma, K.L. "Library in the Fourth Estate." *Indian Library Association Bulletin* 9 (April-June 1973): 54-60.

97. Shoemaker, Ralph J. "Newspaper Library." (letter) *Editor and Publisher* 104 (September 25, 1971): 7.

98. Shoemaker, Ralph J. "Newspaper Library a 'Morgue' Again?" *Editor and Publisher* 97 (September 5, 1964): 48.

99. Simmons, Joseph M. "Archives in the Newspaper Library." Paper presented at the 56th Annual Conference of the Special Libraries Association, Philadelphia, PA, 6-10 June 1965. (ANPA 65-10)

100. Slate, Ted. "A Library or a Morgue?" *D.C. Libraries* 34 (April 1963): 18-22.

101. Smith, Evelyn. "A College Workshop for Small Newspaper Libraries." Paper presented at the 54th Annual Conference of the Special Libraries Association, Denver, CO, 9-13 June 1963. (ANPA 63-13)

102. Smith, (Major General) "The ANPA Looks at the Newspaper Library." Paper presented at the 56th Annual Conference of the Special Libraries Association, Philadelphia, PA, 6-10 June 1965. (ANPA 65-11)

103. Smythe, Eric J.C. "The Library of A Newspaper." Library Association Record 50 (August 1948): 207-210.

104. Snowhite, Morton. "Techniques Used in Newspaper Libraries." Master's thesis, Drexel Institute of Technology, 1950.

105. Snyder, R. Seely. "The Newspaper Library in Philadelphia and Cleveland." Master's thesis, Western Reserve University, June 14, 1950.

106. "Special Pre-Convention Seminar for Smaller Newspapers' Libraries and New Librarians." Paper presented at the 64th Annual Conference of the Special Libraries Association, Pittsburgh, PA, 10-14 June 1973. (ANPA 73-11)

107. Stevens, Robert. "Where Have All the Old Morgues Gone?" Show-Me Libraries 35 (December 1983): 11-14.

108. Sullivan, Bernice. "Photo Composition (Cold Type) and the Library." Paper presented at the 65th Annual Conference of the Special Libraries Association, Toronto, Canada, 9-13 June 1974. (ANPA 74-7)

109. Sykes, Cyril. "Improving the Image of the Newspaper Library." Paper presented at the 55th Annual Conference of the Special Libraries Association, St. Louis, MO, 7-11 June 1964. (ANPA 64-12)

110. "Technical Center." (ANPA's Technical Library) Editor and Publisher 116 (June 18, 1983): 13-14.

111. "30 Librarians Attend Seminar." Editor and Publisher 100 (January 28, 1967): 48.

112. Thorogood, Horace. "The Newspaper Office Library." Library Review 96 (Winter 50): 488-491.

113. Trimble, Kathleen. "Newspaper Libraries -- Automated and Non-Automated Systems: Non-Automated Approaches." *Editor and Publisher* 113 (January 12, 1980): 16-17.

114. Tucker, D.S. "Newspaper Library and Its Service." *SLA Georgia Chapter Bulletin* 2 (August 1956): 5-6.

115. "U.S. Librarian Organizes Files for Viet Service." *Editor and Publisher* 99 (September 17, 1966): 54.

116. Visconty, Jean. "Science Information Services Can Cooperate with Newspaper Libraries." Paper presented at the 56th Annual Conference of the Special Libraries Association, Philadelphia, PA, 6-10 June 1965. (ANPA 65-12)

117. Vormelker, Rose L. "Goals to Be Reached in Newspaper Libraries Through Standards." *Special Libraries* 53 (December 1962): 579-585. Paper presented at the 53rd Annual Conference of the Special Libraries Association, Washington, DC, 27-31 May 1962. (ANPA 62-10)

118. Walker, Joy M. "A Library of Clippings and Photos." *North Carolina Libraries* 25 (Summer 1967): 84-86.

119. Weems, Eddie J. "Morgues Aren't Dead." *Library Journal* 80 (November 1, 1955): 2413-2416.

120. Weems, Eddie J. "Newspaper Libraries; Current Trends." *Special Libraries* 45 (December 1954): 414-415.

121. Weems, Eddie J. "A Study of American Newspaper Libraries." Master's thesis, Florida State University, August 1954.

122. Weiller, Herman E. "Newspaper Library." *Stechert-Hafner News* 10 (January 1956): 53-55.

123. Welch, Mary. "Problems of Moving a Newspaper Library." Paper presented at the 53rd Annual Conference of the Special Libraries Association, Washington, DC, 27-31 May 1962. (ANPA 62-11)

124. Whatmore, Geoffrey. "Daylight in the Mortuary." Librarian and Book World 40 (January 1951): 5-6.

125. Whatmore, Geoffrey. "How the Newspaper Library Does It." Library Review 109 (Spring 1954): 270-273.

126. Whatmore, Geoffrey. The Modern News Library; Documentation of Current Affairs in Newspaper and Broadcasting Libraries. London: The Library Association, 1978.

127. Whatmore, Geoffrey. News Information: The Organization of Press Cuttings in the Libraries of Newspapers and Broadcasting Services. London: Crosby Lockwood, 1965.

128. Whatmore, Geoffrey. "News Libraries and Collections." In Encyclopedia of Library and Information Science, edited by Allen Kent, Harold Lancour, and Jay E. Daily, 465-474. New York: Marcel Dekker, Inc., 1976.

129. Whatmore, Geoffrey. "Newspaper Libraries." (letter) The London Times, 4 July 1974, p. 17.

130. Whatmore, Geoffrey. "Why Newspaper Libraries?" North West Newsletter no. 16 (July 1952): 1-2.

131. Whitworth, Bess. "The Modern Library is Replacing the Old 'Morgue' as a Vital Part of Every Newspaper." Paper presented at the 52nd Annual Conference of the Special Libraries Association, San Francisco, CA, May 28 - June 1 1961. (ANPA 61-4)

132. Whitworth, Bess. "The Value of a Technical Library." Paper presented at the 53rd Annual Conference of the Special Libraries Association, Washington, DC, 27-31 May 1962. (ANPA 62-12)

133. Williams, Charles R. "Role of the Newspaper Library." Master's thesis, University of Mississippi, June 1957.

134. "Williams File at Columbia is Modernized." *Editor and Publisher* 81 (May 29, 1948): 28.

135. Wood, Harry G. "Seminar Points Index Finger at Libraries' Service, Space." *Editor and Publisher* 104 (March 27, 1971): 13-14.

136. Wright, Palmer H. "Efficient, Up-to-Date Libraries Are Not Costly." *Editor and Publisher* 72 (September 2, 1939): 27.

137. Wright, Walter. "Investigative Reporting and Newspaper Libraries." Paper presented at the 70th Annual Conference of the Special Libraries Association, Honolulu, HI, 9-14 June 1979. (ANPA 79-8)

138. Zimmerman, Peter J. "Libraries Behind the News." *Library Journal* 90 (October 15, 1965): 4291-4295.

THE HISTORY OF NEWSPAPER LIBRARIES

139. "Agnes Henebry, New Chairman of Librarians." *Editor and Publisher* 81 (June 19, 1948): 72.

140. Arany, Lawrence A. "*Indianapolis Star* and *News* Library: History and Services." *Library Occurrent* 21 (June 1965): 243-244.

141. "Attendance at Librarians' Parley Urged." *Editor and Publisher* 87 (March 27, 1954): 40.

142. Axelrod, Helene Bernice. "The History, Development, and Organization of the *New York Times* Library, and Contribution of the *Times* to Scholarship." Master's thesis, Southern Connecticut State College, 1965.

143. Bittinger, Betty Jo. "The *Arkansas Gazette* Library." *Arkansas Libraries* 16 (October 1959): 11.

144. "*Boston Globe* Starts New Resource Center Project." *Editor and Publisher* 112 (June 2, 1979): 24, 38.

145. Brandenburg, George A. "Librarians Hear How to Better Service." *Editor and Publisher* 80 (June 14, 1947): 12, 65.

146. Burness, Jack K. "An Appeal to M.E.: Librarians Profit from Conventions." *Editor and Publisher* 95 (February 3, 1962): 62.

147. Burness, Jack K. "Today's News Makes Tomorrow's History." *D.C. Libraries* 28 (July 1957): 9-11.

148. Burness, Jack K.; Clement Vitek; and Milton Prensky. "Proposed Standards for Newspaper Libraries." *Special Libraries* 51 (November 1960): 501-504. Paper presented at the 51st Annual Conference of the Special Libraries Association, Cleveland, OH, 5-8 June 1960.

149. Calixto-Aunario, Jesusa. "The Library of the Manila Daily Bulletin." ASLP Bulletin 12 (June 1966): 29-31.

150. Castro, Leticia A. "The Special Collection of the Manila Times." ASLP Bulletin 7 (September 1961): 91-92.

151. Clark, Wesley C. "Talk by Dr. Wesley C. Clark, Dean School of Journalism, Newhouse Communications Center, Syracuse University." Paper presented at the 56th Annual Conference of the Special Libraries Association, Philadelphia, PA, 6-10 June 1965. (ANPA 65-2)

152. Clemente-Carpio, Conchita. "The Manila Chronicle Library." ASLP Bulletin 12 (June 1966): 27-29.

153. Crachi, Rocco. "Production of Chapter and Division Bulletins, SLA." Paper presented at the 62nd Annual Conference of the Special Libraries Association, San Francisco, CA, 6-10 June 1971. (ANPA 71-7)

154. Curtiss, Frances E. "Library of the Detroit News." Wilson Library Bulletin 16 (November 1941): 250-251.

155. "Dailies' Librarians Hear Work Praised; James E. Craig, N.Y. Sun Editorial Writer, Pays Radio Tribute at Special Convention in New York." Editor and Publisher 70 (June 19, 1937): 55.

156. Faylona, Yolanda T. "The Phillippines Herald Library." ASLP Bulletin 12 (June 1966): 31-33.

157. Feldmeir, Daryle. "An Inconclusion." Paper presented at the 57th Annual Conference of the Special Libraries Association, Minneapolis, MN, May 29-June 2 1966. (ANPA 66-3)

158. "Ferger Tells Librarians Readers Like Courage." Editor and Publisher 87 (May 22, 1954): 9. Presentation at the 45th Annual Conference of the Special Libraries Association, Cincinnati, OH, 17-22 May 1954.

159. Ferguson, George V. "Remarks by George V. Ferguson, Editor Emeritus of the Montreal Star." Paper presented at the 60th Annual Conference of the Special Libraries Association, Montreal, Canada, 1-5 June 1969. (ANPA 69-2)

160. Foster, Paul P. "The Library of the Philadelphia Inquirer - A Model Newspaper Library." Special Libraries 36 (April 1945): 116-119.

161. Foster, Paul P. "The Philadelphia Inquirer Library." Bulletin of the Special Libraries Council of Philadelphia and Vicinity 9 (September 1942): 1-4.

162. "Four Librarians Given Roll of Honor Awards at Atlanta Conference." Editor and Publisher 114 (July 11, 1981): 44.

163. Friendly, Alfred. "Remarks at the Presentation of the First Jack K. Burness Memorial Award." Paper presented at the 56th Annual Conference of the Special Libraries Association, Philadelphia, PA, 6-10 June 1965. (ANPA 65-4)

164. Furman, Sophia. "Chicago Journal of Commerce." Illinois Libraries 29 (December 1947): 458-459.

165. Giovine, S. Richard. "Library is Born in Modern Times." Special Libraries 32 (September 1941): 254-255.

166. Goodman, Marian M. "In San Francisco: Newspaper Libraries Date from 1906." Editor and Publisher 94 (February 11, 1961): 42-43.

167. Hall, Sandy. "Report of the Committee on Educational Activities and Professional Development." Report presented at the 68th Annual Conference of the Special Libraries Association, New York, NY, 5-9 June 1977. (ANPA 77-4)

168. Henebry, Agnes C. "Decatur Herald-Review Library." Illinois Libraries 14 (July 1932): 65-66.

169. Henebry, Agnes C. "Herald and Review Library." Illinois Libraries 36 (February 1954): 77-80.

170. Inman, Robert. "Remarks by Robert Inman." Remarks made at the 57th Annual Conference of the Special Libraries Association, Minneapolis, MN, May 29 - June 1 1966. (ANPA 66-4)

171. "The International Scene: News and Abstracts - Archives of the Times." *American Archivist* 39 (July 1976): 383-384.

172. Ippolito, Andrew V. "Automation Committee Report." Report presented at the 68th Annual Conference of the Special Libraries Association, New York, NY, 5-9 June 1977. (ANPA 77-6)

173. Jacobus, Alma. "*Time* Library in War Time; Abridged." *Special Libraries* 31 (July-August 1940): 234-245.

174. Jessup, Lee Cheney. "Newspaper Library for *The Nashville Banner*." *Tennessee Librarian* 10 (January 1958): 39-40.

175. Johnson, Josephine R. "The *Courier-Journal* and *Louisville Times* Library: A Sketch." *Kentucky Library Association Bulletin* 38 (Spring 1974): 9-11.

176. "Kentucky." *Southeastern Librarian* 28 (Winter 1978): 263.

177. King, Roy T. "*Post Dispatch* Library Geared to Deadlines." *Show-Me Libraries* 20 (July 1969): 1+.

178. Kumer, Mildred E. "The Library Behind the *Detroit News*." *Junior Librarian* 1 (July-October 1940): 77-80.

179. Lewis, Chester Milton. "A Century of Service." *Library Journal* 76 (September 15, 1951): 1371-1374.

180. Lewis, Chester Milton. "Librarians Invited to Know-How Parley." *Editor and Publisher* 86 (May 9, 1953): 46.

181. Lewis, Chester Milton. "What Price Bulletins?" *Special Libraries* 44 (March 1953): 111-112.

182. "Lewis Heads Newspaper Librarians." *Editor and Publisher* 85 (May 31, 1952): 12.

183. "Librarians Begin Study of Standards." *Editor and Publisher* 93 (June 11, 1960): 73.

184. "Librarians Elect Ippolito of *Newsday*." *Editor and Publisher* 101 (July 6, 1968): 30.

185. "Librarians Get Into Row Over Name Change." *Editor and Publisher* 80 (June 21, 1947): 48.

186. "Librarians Plan Meeting in June." *Editor and Publisher* 101 (April 6, 1968): 20.

187. "Librarians Plan 25th Meeting Week of June 6." *Editor and Publisher* 81 (May 22, 1948): 68.

188. "Librarians Start Burness Award to Honor Own." *Editor and Publisher* 97 (September 26, 1964): 74.

189. "Librarians Study Service, Microfilm." *Editor and Publisher* 84 (June 23, 1951): 71.

190. "Library and Reference Collection of the *New York Journal-American* Given to the University of Texas." *Texas Library Journal* 44 (Summer 1968): 75.

191. "Library Transferred to Index Department." *Editor and Publisher* 100 (October 14, 1967): 28.

192. "Louisville Day-May 21, 1954; Post Convention Program Highlights." *Special Libraries* 45 (April 1954): 170-171.

193. McCormick, Robert R. "*Chicago Tribune* Library." *Illinois Libraries* 37 (January 1955): 10-13.

194. Miller, Diane. "Morgue Is Not Dead." *Illinois Libraries* 62 (March 1980): 250-252.

195. "New Morgue Site Sought for Defunct Newspapers." *Editor and Publisher* 116 (May 14, 1983): 36.

196. "*N.Y. News* Ends Library Space Jam." *Editor and Publisher* 102 (January 11, 1969): 56.

197. "NYU Receives *Tribune's* Morgue." *Wilson Library Bulletin* 42 (December 1967): 361.

198. "Newspaper Division Veterans Honored." *Editor and Publisher* 87 (May 15, 1954): 68.

199. "Newspaper Librarians Convention Discussions." Report of the 53rd Annual Conference of the Special Libraries Association, Washington, DC, 27-31 May 1962. (ANPA 62-13)

200. "Newspaper Librarians Convention Discussions." Report of the 54th Annual Conference of the Special Libraries Association, Denver, CO, 9-13 June 1963. (ANPA 63-14)

201. "Newspaper Librarians Convention Discussions and Newspaper Libraries Clinic." (transcript) Report of the 55th Annual Conference of the Special Libraries Association, 7-11 June 1964. (ANPA 64-3)

202. "Newspaper Librarians Convention Discussion." Report of the 56th Annual Conference of the Special Libraries Association, Philadelphia, PA, 6-10 June 1965. (ANPA 65-15)

203. "Newspaper Librarians Convention Discussions." Report of the 57th Annual Conference of the Special Libraries Association, Minneapolis, MN, May 29 - June 2 1966. (ANPA 66-10)

204. "Newspaper Librarians Conference Discussions." Report of the 58th Annual Conference of the Special Libraries Association, New York, NY, May 28 - June 1 1967. (ANPA 67-6)

205. "Newspaper Librarians Conference Discussions, Transcript of." Report of the 61st Annual Conference of the Special Libraries Association, Detroit, MI, 7-11 June 1970. (ANPA 70-8)

206. "Newspaper Librarians Conference Discussions, Transcript of." Report of the 62nd Annual Conference of the Special Libraries Association, San Francisco, CA, 6-10 June 1971. (ANPA 71-6)

207. "Newspaper Morgues Are Given Away." *Editor and Publisher* 100 (November 11, 1967): 12.

208. Philip, D.M. "*The Star* Reference Library." *South African Libraries* 12 (July 1944): 5-6.

209. "Program to Raise Status of Library." *Editor and Publisher* 93 (July 9, 1960): 64.

210. "Quiet New Morgue Front Tightens Record Control." *Times Talk* 7 (October 1953): 1.

211. Reitman, Jo. "The Real Story of the Newspapers, Inc. Library." *Wisconsin Library Bulletin* 78 (Fall 1983): 105-107.

212. "Research Duties of Librarians Are Expanded." *Editor and Publisher* 83 (June 24, 1950): 61.

213. Rupp, Carla Marie. "Everything Is Tape-Recorded: *National Enquirer's* Research Department Confirms Accuracy." *Editor and Publisher* 111 (April 29, 1978): 112-114.

214. "SLA Newspaper Division Standards Committee Report, 1962." Paper presented at the 53rd Annual Conference of the Special Libraries Association, Washington, DC, 27-31 May 1962. (ANPA 62-7)

215. Sanger, Chester W. "*Christian Science Monitor* Library." *SLA Boston Chapter Bulletin* 26 (November 1959): 7.

216. Sanger, Chester W. "Report of the Newspaper Division Standards Committee, 1962-63." Paper presented at the 54th Annual Conference of the Special Libraries Association, Denver, CO, 9-13 June 1963. (ANPA 63-15)

217. Sardella, Mark. "*Boston Globe* Library." *Bay State Librarian* 69 (Winter 1980): 12-16.

218. Shoemaker, Ralph J. "Fifty Years of the Newspaper Division." Paper presented at the 64th Annual Conference of the Special Libraries Association, Pittsburgh, PA, 10-14 June 1973.

219. Shoemaker, Ralph J. "Fond Recollection of Early SLA Days." *Special Libraries* 69 (August 1978): 311-312.

220. Simmons, Joseph M. "The Library of the Chicago *Sun-Times Daily News*." *Illinois Libraries* 45 (November 1963): 503-508.

221. Simmons, Joseph M. "Merging of the *Chicago Sun-Times* and *Daily News* Libraries." Paper presented at the 55th Annual Conference of the Special Libraries Association, St. Louis, MO, 7-11 June 1964. (ANPA 64-10)

222. *60th Anniversary -- Commemorative Publication of the Newspaper Division of the Special Libraries Association, 1924 - 1984*. St. Louis, MO: St. Louis Post-Dispatch, 1984.

223. Slate, Joseph Evans. "*Journal-American* Morgue." *Library Chronicle* 2 (November 1970): 82-89.

224. Smutny, Charles T. "*Chicago Tribune* Library." *Illinois Libraries* 30 (February 1948): 103-104.

225. "Some Notes on the *Montreal-Star* Library Routine." Paper presented at the 60th Annual Conference of the Special Libraries Association, Montreal, Canada, 1-5 June 1969. (ANPA 69-12)

226. Stolberg, Charles. "Librarians Elect Mrs. Lee Jessup of Nashville." *Editor and Publisher* 86 (July 4, 1953): 40.

227. "Subject Heading Reports and Discussions." Presented at the 57th Annual Conference of the Special Libraries Association, Minneapolis, MN, May 29 - June 2 1966. (ANPA 66-11)

228. Surace, Cecily J. *Editorial Library: User Survey*. Arlington, VA: ERIC Document Reproduction Service, ED 197 726, 1980.

229. Thomas, Alfred. "In Our Libraries: The *Arkansas Gazette* News Library." *Arkansas Libraries* 40 (September 1983): 27-28.

230. Thomas, Lou. "The *State-Times--Morning Advocate* Newspaper Library." *Louisiana Library Association Bulletin* 33 (Winter 1971): 109-112.

231. "Transcript of Newspaper Librarians Conference Discussions." Report of the 60th Annual Conference of the Special Libraries Association, Montreal, Canada, 1-5 June 1969. (ANPA 69-11)

232. Whatmore, Geoffrey. "A New Newspaper Library." *Library Review* 22 (Summer 1970): 311-313.

233. Whatmore, Geoffrey. "*The Manchester Guardian* Library." *Manchester Review* 6 (Autumn 1953): 473-476.

234. "Where the Past Is Prologue: Library Has 'Tomorrow Look'." *Editor and Publisher* 102 (October 25, 1969): 17.

235. Wolcoff, P. "Organization and Functioning of the *New York Times* Clipping Files." Master's thesis, Pratt Institute Library School, 1954.

236. Woodhouse, Renie. "Newspaper Library Work." *South African Libraries* 16 (July 1948): 26-29.

237. "World of Print: *New York Herald Tribune* Morgue." *Library Journal* 92 (December 15, 1967): 4461.

238. Wright, Palmer H. "Efficient, Up-to-Date Libraries Are Not Costly." *Editor and Publisher* 72 (September 2, 1939): 27.

ORGANIZATION AND ADMINISTRATION OF NEWSPAPER LIBRARIES

239. Andrews, Elliott E. "The Providence *Journal* News Library Manual." Paper presented at the 52nd Annual Conference of the Special Libraries Association, San Francisco, CA, May 28-June 1 1961. (ANPA 61-1)

240. Andrews, Elliott E. "This Works for Us . . . Staff Organization." *Special Libraries* 54 (March 1963): 162. Abstracted from paper presented at the 53rd Annual Conference of the Special Libraries Association, Washington, DC, 27-31 May 1962. (ANPA 62-1)

241. Betty, Samuel. "Effective Employee Communication." Paper presented at the 67th Annual Conference of the Special Libraries Association, Denver, CO, 6-10 June 1976. (ANPA 76-2)

242. Carter, J. Howard. "Libel Law Pertaining to Newspapers." *Special Libraries* 32 (September 1941): 256-258. Paper presented at the 33rd Annual Conference of the Special Libraries Association, Hartford, CT, 16-19 June 1941.

243. Graham, Evarts A. "*St. Louis Post-Dispatch* In-Plant Training Program." Paper presented at the 55th Annual Conference of the Special Libraries Association, St. Louis, MO, 7-11 June 1964. (ANPA 64-4)

244. Greene, Elwin S. "Newspaper Library Personnel Problems." Paper presented at the 54th Annual Conference of the Special Libraries Association, Denver, CO, 9-13 June 1963. (ANPA 63-7)

245. Hall, Sandy. "Personnel." Paper presented at the 66th Annual Conference of the Special Libraries Association, Chicago, IL, 8-12 June 1975. (ANPA 75-3)

246. "Insurance for Newspaper Libraries." *Special Libraries* 57 (February 1966): 115-116.

247. Isaacs, Bob D. "Performance Evaluation and Motivation." Paper presented at the 75th Annual Conference of the Special Libraries Association, New York, NY, 9-14 June 1984. (ANPA 84-4)

248. Isaacs, Bob D. "The Small Newspaper Library Budget in Comparison with a Medium-Sized Newspaper Library Budget." Paper presented at the 68th Annual Conference of the Special Libraries Association, New York, NY, 5-9 June 1977. (ANPA 77-7)

249. Johnson, Josephine. "Library Personnel." Paper presented at the 65th Annual Conference of the Special Libraries Association, Toronto, Canada, 9-13 June 1974. (ANPA 74-3)

250. Kirsh, Julie. "Managing the Newspaper Library and Its Collections." Paper presented at the 76th Annual Conference of the Special Libraries Association, Winnipeg, Canada, 8-13 June 1985. (ANPA)

251. Kirsh, Julie. "Staff Management in a News Library." Paper presented at the 76th Annual Conference of the Special Libraries Association, Winnipeg, Canada, 8-13 June 1985. (ANPA)

252. Koenig, Michael E.D. "Budgeting for the Newspaper Library." Paper presented at the 69th Annual Conference of the Special Libraries Association, Kansas City, MO, 10-15 June 1978. (ANPA 78-1).

253. Lathrop, Mary Lou. "Library Management Through Change." Paper presented at the 66th Annual Conference of the Special Libraries Association, Chicago, IL, 8-12 June 1975. (ANPA 75-4)

254. "Laws Ruled Unconstitutional: Illinois Judge Kills News File Subpoenas." Editor and Publisher 103 (May 30, 1970): 46.

255. Lindsay, Carol. "Administration of the Small Newspaper Library." Paper presented at the 68th Annual Conference of the Special Libraries Association, New York, NY, 5-9 June 1977. (ANPA 77-8)

256. Lindsay, Carol. "Management, Budget, Personnel, Communication." Paper presented at the 71st Annual Conference of the Special Libraries Association, Washington, DC, 7-12 June 1980. (ANPA 80-6)

257. Luedtke, Kurt. "Future of Newspaper Libraries - A Management View." Paper presented at the 66th Annual Conference of the Special Libraries Association, Chicago, IL, 8-12 June 1975. (ANPA 75-5)

258. McCarthy, Joseph F. "Library Files - Open or Closed to Readers." Paper presented at the 65th Annual Conference of the Special Libraries Association, Toronto, Canada, 9-13 June 1974. (ANPA 74-4)

259. "Manual Explains Library Methods and Systems." Editor and Publisher 108 (June 28, 1975): 26.

260. Martin, Homer E., Jr. "How Newspaper Librarians Use Committees to Bring About Change." Paper presented at the 72nd Annual Conference of the Special Libraries Association, Atlanta, GA, 13-18 June 1981. (ANPA 81-6)

261. Martin, Homer E., Jr. "Newspaper Library Administration." Paper presented at the 67th Annual Conference of the Special Libraries Association, Denver, CO, 6-10 June 1976. (ANPA 76-7).

262. Michaels, Andrea, and David Michaels. "Space Planning for the Newspaper Library." Paper presented at the 75th Annual Conference of the Special Libraries Association, New York, NY, 9-14 June 1984. (ANPA 84-8)

263. Miniter, John J. "Library Management by Objectives: Will It Succeed? (Includes Dallas Morning News Statement)." Paper presented at the 69th Annual Conference of the Special Libraries Association, Kansas City, MO, 10-15 June 1978. (ANPA 78-4)

264. "Newspaper Library Basics Seminar." Report of seminar held at the 68th Annual Conference of the Special Libraries Association, New York, NY, 5-9 June 1977. (ANPA 77-17)

265. Oppedahl, Alison. "Newspaper Library Budgeting." Paper presented at the 68th Annual Conference of the Special Libraries Association, New York, NY, 5-9 June 1977. (ANPA 77-9)

266. Orgain, Marian M. "Newspaper Library Budgeting." Special Libraries 55 (January 1964): 30-33. Paper presented at the 54th Annual Conference of the Special Libraries Association, Denver, CO, 9-13 June 1963. (ANPA 63-9)

267. Orgain, Marian M. "Problems of Reorganizing a Newspaper Library." Special Libraries 53 (December 1962): 586-589. Paper presented at the 53rd Annual Conference of the Special Libraries Association, Washington, DC, 27-31 May 1962. (ANPA 62-4)

268. Parsley, Leslie. "The Birth of a Manual." Paper presented at the 68th Annual Conference of the Special Libraries Association, New York, NY, 5-9 June 1977. (ANPA 77-10)

269. Perkins, Don. "Problems in 'Self-Service' Libraries -- Subject Heading Control, Circulation, After-Hours Security." Paper presented at the 72nd Annual Conference of the Special Libraries Association, Atlanta, GA, 13-18 June 1981. (ANPA 81-9)

270. Petersen, Agnes J. "Personnel: A Symposium; Abridged." *Special Libraries* 31 (July-August 1940): 237-239. Paper presented at the 32nd Annual Conference of the Special Libraries Association, Indianapolis, IN, 3-6 June 1940.

271. Pettit, Ford M. "Newspaper Library and the Five-day Week." *Special Libraries Association Proceedings* 1 (1938): 78-79. Paper presented at the 30th Annual Conference of the Special Libraries Association, Pittsburgh, PA, 7-11 June 1938.

272. Ploch, Richard. "Library Management/Library - Newsroom Communication." Paper presented at the 73rd Annual Conference of the Special Libraries Association, Detroit, MI, 5-10 June 1982. (ANPA 82-5)

273. Richards, Dargan A. "Recognizing Your Limits." Paper presented at the 72nd Annual Conference of the Special Libraries Association, Atlanta, GA, 13-18 June 1982. (ANPA 81-10)

274. Rouse, J. Michael. "One Editor's Advice to Librarians." Paper presented at the 74th Annual Conference of the Special Libraries Association, New Orleans, LA, 4-9 June 1983. (ANPA 83-3)

275. Russell, Beverly; Sharon Reeves; and Gail McLaughlin. "The Effects of Automation on Your Library Staff." Program presented at the 76th Annual Conference of the Special Libraries Association, Winnipeg, Canada, 8-13 June 1985.

276. Scofield, James S. *Information Service*. Arlington, VA: ERIC Document Reproduction Service, ED 107 277, 1973. Paper presented at the 64th Annual Conference of the Special Libraries Association, Pittsburgh, PA, 10-14 June 1973. (ANPA 73-7)

277. Scofield, James S. "Public Service." Paper presented at the 66th Annual Conference of the Special Libraries Association, Chicago, IL, 8-12 June 1975. (ANPA 75-8)

278. Semonche, Barbara P. "Staff Management in Small Newspaper Libraries." Paper presented at the 72nd Annual Conference of the Special Libraries Association, Atlanta, GA, 13-18 June 1981. (ANPA 81-11)

279. Semonche, Barbara P. "Staff Management in Small Newspaper Libraries." Paper presented at the 73rd Annual Conference of the Special Libraries Association, Detroit, MI, 5-10 June 1982. (ANPA 82-9)

280. Sharma, K.L. "Newspaper Library Acquisitions--Policy and Procedures." <u>Indian Library Association Bulletin</u> 12 (January - March 1976): 30-34.

281. Thomas, Lou. "Managing the Library." Paper presented at the 75th Annual Conference of the Special Libraries Association, New York, NY, 9-14 June 1984. (ANPA 84-11)

282. Thomas, Lou. "Special Problems of the Small Library." Paper presented at the 65th Annual Conference of the Special Libraries Association, Toronto, Canada, 9-13 June 1974. (ANPA 74-8)

283. Tiffen, Pauline, and James F. Tiffen. "I'm on Deadline: Coping with Stress in a News Library Environment." Paper presented at the 76th Annual Conference of the Special Libraries Association, Winnipeg, Canada, 8-13 June 1985.

284. Trimble, Kathleen. "User Communication in Special Libraries." Paper presented at the 69th Annual Conference of the Special Libraries Association, Kansas City, MO, 10-15 June 1978. (ANPA 78-5)

285. "Weeding Libraries Takes Judgement." <u>Editor and Publisher</u> 99 (February 12, 1966): 34.

286. Wells, Chris. "Library Equipment Survey Results." Paper presented at the 75th Annual Conference of the Special Libraries Association, New York, NY, 9-14 June 1984. (ANPA 84-13)

287. Wixom, Sharen Elizabeth, and Lee S. Wixom. "Cost and Work Saving Ideas." Paper presented at the 65th Annual Conference of the Special Libraries Association, Toronto, Canada, 9-13 June 1974. (ANPA 74-10)

288. Wood, Ellen. "Librarians May Feel Impact of Libel Decision (Herbert vs. Lando)." <u>Editor and Publisher</u> 112 (July 21, 1979): 11.

CLASSIFICATION AND FILING

289. Abramson, Abe. "Coping With the Problems of Near and Far Eastern Names." Paper presented at the 60th Annual Conference of the Special Libraries Association, Montreal, Canada, 1-5 June 1969. (ANPA 69-1)

290. "*Akron Beacon Journal* Topical Clip Index." Paper presented at the 58th Annual Conference of the Special Libraries Association, New York, NY, May 28 - June 1. (ANPA 67-1)

291. Andrews, Elliott E. "The *Providence Journal* News Library Manual." Paper presented at the 52nd Annual Conference of the Special Libraries Association, San Francisco, CA, May 28 - June 1 1961. (ANPA 61-1)

292. Andrews, Elliott E. "This Works for Us . . . Staff Organization." *Special Libraries* 54 (March 1963): 162. Abstracted from paper presented at the 53rd Annual Conference of the Special Libraries Association, Washington, DC, 27-31 May 1962. (ANPA 62-1)

293. "Automated News Clipping, Indexing, and Retrieval System (ANCIRS)." *Journal of Library Automation* 7 (September 1974): 235.

294. Bavakutty, M. "Organization of Newspaper Cuttings." *International Library Movement* 2 (1980): 86-90.

295. Beegan, John F. "Subject - Clipping Files." Paper presented at the 66th Annual Conference of the Special Libraries Association, Chicago, IL, 8-12 June 1975. (ANPA 75-1)

296. Beegan, John F.; Helen Everts; and Charles Martyn. "Marking the Newspaper." Paper presented at the 64th Annual Conference of the Special Libraries Association, Pittsburgh, PA, 10-14 June. (ANPA 73-1)

297. Breuer, M.H. "*Herald-Traveler* Picture Files." *SLA Picture Division Picturescope* 5 (October 1957): 22-23.

298. Briscoe, Ellis. "Subject Headings." Paper presented at the 76th Annual Conference of the Special Libraries Association, Winnipeg, Canada, 8-13 June 1985. (ANPA)

299. Chase, William D. "The Newspaper Photo Library." Paper presented at the 68th Annual Conference of the Special Libraries Association, New York, NY, 5-9 June 1977. (ANPA 77-1)

300. Christian Science Publishing Society Research Library. "Rules for Biographical Filing." Paper presented at the 54th Annual Conference of the Special Libraries Association, Denver, CO, 9-13 June 1963. (ANPA 63-2)

301. "Clips on Computer Make Retrieval Work a Snap." Editor and Publisher 109 (June 26, 1976): 13.

302. Conklin, Florina. "Subject Headings for Newspaper Libraries." Paper presented at the 56th Annual Conference of the Special Libraries Association, Philadelphia, PA, 6-10 June 1965. (ANPA 65-3)

303. Criswell, James. "Study of Newspaper Library Pictures." Paper presented at the 63rd Annual Conference of the Special Libraries Association, Boston, MA, 4-8 June 1972. (ANPA 72-7)

304. Cushman, Robert. "Conservation Problems and Suggested Practical Techniques for Dealing with Extremely Large Collections of 20th Century Photographs." Paper presented at the 73rd Annual Conference of the Special Libraries Association, Detroit, MI, 5-10 June 1982. (ANPA 82-3)

305. Eggleston, Alma. "Life Picture Collection." Special Libraries 45 (September 1954): 284-287.

306. Finberg, Howard; Barbara Newcomb; and James S. Scofield. "Serving the Graphics Needs of the Newsroom." Program presented at the 76th Annual Conference of the Special Libraries Association, Winnipeg, Canada, 8-13 June 1985.

307. Fingland, Geoffrey; Ernest Perez; and Lou Thomas. *Library Files; Open or Closed to Readers?* Arlington, VA: ERIC Document Reproduction Services, ED 107 276, June 1974. Paper presented at the 65th Annual Conference of the Special Libraries Association, Toronto, Canada, 9-13 June 1974.

308. Foley, Kathy. "Newspaper Clipping Files." Paper presented at the 71st Annual Conference of the Special Libraries Association, Washington, DC, 7-12 June 1980. (ANPA 80-3)

309. Fomerand, Raissa. "Newspaper Clipping File." *Unabashed Librarian* no. 10 (Winter 1974): 7.

310. Frankland, John R. "Corrections and Revisions of Clipping and Photo Files." New York: American Newspaper Publishers Association, 1968.

311. Gibbs-Smith, C.H. "The Hulton Picture Post Library." *Journal of Documentation* 6 (March 1950): 12-24.

312. Giovine, S. Richard. "Master List of European War Subject Headings; Abridged." *Special Libraries* 31 (July-August 1940): 231. Paper presented at the 32nd Annual Conference of the Special Libraries Association, Indianapolis, IN, 3-6 June 1940.

313. Grayland, Eugene Charles. *The Newspaper Reference Library and the Filing and Uses of Press Clippings.* Auckland, New Zealand: Colenso Press, 1950.

314. Harris, Vivian. "Methods of Filing Newspaper Clippings." Paper presented at the 54th Annual Conference of the Special Libraries Association, Denver, CO, 9-13 June 1963. (ANPA 63-8)

315. Harrison, Alice W. "Conservation of Library Materials: Clip No. 11: Newspaper Clipping Files." *Atlantic Provinces Library Association Bulletin* 43 (September 1979): 6.

316. Henebry, Agnes C. "Preservation of Photographs on Microfilm: An Experiment." *Special Libraries* 47 (December 1956): 451-454.

317. Hill, Joy. "Graphic Arts--Processing and Filing (Newspaper Basics Seminar)." Paper presented at the 67th Annual Conference of the Special Libraries Association, Denver, CO, 6-10 June 1976. (ANPA 76-5)

318. Hill, Joy, and others. Photo Storage and Retrieval. Arlington, VA: ERIC Document Reproduction Service, ED 107 278, June 1973. Paper presented at the 64th Annual Conference of the Special Libraries Association, Pittsburgh, PA, 10-14 June 1973. (ANPA 73-3)

319. House, Audrey C. "Building a Picture File." Paper presented at the 53rd Annual Conference of the Special Libraries Association, Washington, DC, 27-31 May 1962. (ANPA 62-3)

320. Ivey, Robert. "Subject Headings." Paper presented at the 73rd Annual Conference of the Special Libraries Association, Detroit, MI, 5-10 June 1982. (ANPA 82-10)

321. Janda, Kenneth, and David Gordon. "Microfilm Information Retrieval System for Newspaper Libraries." Special Libraries 61 (January 1970): 33-47. Paper presented at the 60th Annual Conference of the Special Libraries Association, Montreal, Canada, 1-5 June 1969. (ANPA 69-4)

322. Johnson, Josephine. "Subject Headings and the New Library Concepts." Paper presented at the 56th Annual Conference of the Special Libraries Association, Philadelphia, PA, 6-10 June 1965. (ANPA 65-6)

323. King, John. "Problems of Storage and Obsolescence." Aslib Proceedings 25 (June 1973): 202-206. Paper presented at a one-day conference on "The Organization of Modern Newspaper Libraries," London, 23 March 1973.

324. Legett, Anne. "Subject Headings." Paper presented at the 73rd Annual Conference of the Special Libraries Association, Detroit, MI, 5-10 June 1982. (ANPA 82-11)

325. "Librarians Have Need of Filing Code." Editor and Publisher 96 (June 15, 1963): 69. Paper presented at the 54th Annual Conference of the Special Libraries Association, Denver, CO, 9-13 June 1963.

326. Lindsay, Carol. "Clipping Files." Paper presented at the 67th Annual Conference of the Special Libraries Association, Denver, CO, 6-10 June 1976. (ANPA 76-6)

327. Luecke, Camilla P. "Photographic Library Procedure." *Special Libraries* 47 (December 1956): 455-461.

328. Lyon, Bill, Jr., and Harry R. Mecinski. "Picture Problems." Paper presented at the 63rd Annual Conference of the Special Libraries Association, Boston, MA, 4-8 June 1972. (ANPA 72-3)

329. McCarthy, Joseph F. "Graphics." Paper presented at the 66th Annual Conference of the Special Libraries Association, Chicago, IL, 8-12 June 1975. (ANPA 75-6)

330. McDonald, Lany W. "Clipping Files." Paper presented at the 73rd Annual Conference of the Special Libraries Association, Detroit, MI, 5-10 June 1982. (ANPA 82-4)

331. May, Barbara. "*Dallas Morning News* Library Online Authority File." Paper presented at the 71st Annual Conference of the Special Libraries Association, Washington, DC, 7-12 June 1980. (ANPA 80-8)

332. Medley, Nora. "Use of the Computer for Subject Heading List." Paper presented at the 71st Annual Conference of the Special Libraries Association, Washington, DC, 7-12 June 1980. (ANPA 80-9)

333. Moore, Waldo H. "Copyright of Pictorial Material." Paper presented at the 55th Annual Conference of the Special Libraries Association, St. Louis, MO, 7-11 June 1964. (ANPA 64-8)

334. "*New York Times* to Publish Guide for Librarians." *Editor and Publisher* 100 (April 8, 1967): 37.

335. "Newspaper Finds Old Clip Files Can Mean Significant Tax Savings." *Presstime* 4 (December 1982): 10.

336. "Newspaper Morgues Are Given Away." *Editor and Publisher* 100 (November 11, 1967): 12.

337. "Newspaper Picture Files of the *World-Journal-Tribune* to LC." *SLA Picture Division Picturescope* 15 (1967): 89.

338. Oppedahl, Alison, and others. *Will Microfilm and Computers Replace Clippings?* Arlington, VA: ERIC Document Reproduction Service, ED 107 274, June 1974. Paper presented at the 65th Annual Conference of the Special Libraries Association, Toronto, Canada, 9-13 June 1974. (ANPA 74-5)

339. Orcutt, Helen M. "Subject Headings for Newspaper Libraries." Paper presented at the 56th Annual Conference of the Special Libraries Association, Philadelphia, PA, 6-10 June 1965. (ANPA 65-7)

340. Parsley, Leslie. "The Process and Equipment Used in Marking and Filing the Paper." Paper presented at the 66th Annual Conference of the Special Libraries Association, Chicago, IL, 8-12 June 1975. (ANPA 75-7).

341. Perez, Ernest R. "Clipping Files - Process and Equipment." Paper presented at the 67th Annual Conference of the Special Libraries Association, Denver, CO, 6-10 June 1976. (ANPA 76-8).

342. Perez, Ernest R.; Rex Schaeffer; and Joy Walker. "Subject Heading List Using Linedex, Computer Print-Outs, Index Cards and Computer Access." Paper presented at the 64th Annual Conference of the Special Libraries Association, Pittsburgh, PA, 10-14 June 1973. (ANPA 73-5)

343. Pettit, Ford M. "*Detroit News* Photographic Negative Library; Abridged." *Special Libraries* 31 (July-August 1940): 239-240. Paper presented at the 32nd Annual Conference of the Special Libraries Association, Indianapolis, IN, 3-6 June 1940.

344. Pettit, Ford M. "Newspaper Librarians Know There's a War On." *Library Journal* 68 (September 1, 1943): 649-651.

345. Power, Eugene B. "The Use of Sheet Film for Newspaper Clippings." *Special Libraries* 45 (March 1954): 111-114. Paper presented at the 44th Annual Conference of the Special Libraries Association, Toronto, Canada, 22-25 June 1953.

346. Prensky, Milton. "Problems of Reorganizing a Newspaper Library." *Special Libraries* 48 (December 1957): 447-451. Paper presented at the 48th Annual Conference of the Special Libraries Association, Boston, MA, 26-31 May 1957.

347. Prince, Vivian. "Subject Heading Creation and Control." Paper presented at the 59th Annual Conference of the Special Libraries Association, Los Angeles, CA, 2-7 June 1968. (ANPA 68-3)

348. "Quiet New Morgue Front Tightens Record Control." *Times Talk* 7 (October 1953): 1.

349. Raines, Elaine Y. "Clipping Files and Subject Headings." Paper presented at the 75th Annual Conference of the Special Libraries Association, New York, NY, 9-14 June 1984. (ANPA 84-9)

350. Rhydwen, David A. "The Application of Microphotography to Newspaper Clippings." *Special Libraries* 55 (January 1964): 28-30. Paper presented at the 54th Annual Conference of the Special Libraries Association, Denver, CO, 9-13 June 1963. (ANPA 63-10)

351. Rhydwen, David A. "Copying Old Negatives." Paper presented at the 60th Annual Conference of the Special Libraries Association, Montreal, Canada, 1-5 June 1969. (ANPA 69-7)

352. Rhydwen, David A. "Filing and Indexing of Negatives at the Toronto *Globe and Mail* Library." Paper presented at the 54th Annual Conference of the Special Libraries Association, Denver, CO, 9-13 June 1963. (ANPA 63-11)

353. Rhydwen, David A. "Indexing of Negatives Using Kalvar at the Toronto *Globe and Mail*." Paper presented at the 57th Annual Conference of the Special Libraries Association, Minneapolis, MN, May 29 - June 2 1966. (ANPA 66-6)

354. Rhydwen, David A. "Microfilming of Clippings Using Kalvar Microfiche." Paper presented at the 57th Annual Conference of the Special Libraries Association, Minneapolis, MN, May 28 - June 1 1967. (ANPA 66-7)

355. Rhydwen, David A. "Subject Headings for Newspaper Libraries." Paper presented at the 56th Annual Conference of the Special Libraries Association, Philadelphia, PA, 6-10 June 1965. (ANPA 65-8)

356. Riker, Elaine M. "Microfilming Newspaper Clippings." Special Libraries 56 (November 1965): 655-656. Paper presented at the 56th Annual Conference of the Special Libraries Association, Philadelphia, PA, 6-10 June 1965. (ANPA 65-9)

357. Sanger, Chester W. "How the Christian Science Monitor Files Foreign Names." Paper presented at the 60th Annual Conference of the Special Libraries Association, Montreal, Canada, 1-5 June 1969. (ANPA 69-8)

358. Sanger, Chester W. "Rules for Biographical Filing - General Rules for Foreign Names." Paper presented at the 60th Annual Conference of the Special Libraries Association, Montreal, Canada, 1-5 June 1969. (ANPA 69-9)

359. Sausedo, Ann. "Subject Classification." Paper presented at the 65th Annual Conference of the Special Libraries Association, Toronto, Canada, 9-13 June 1974. (ANPA 74-6)

360. Schaeffer, Rex. "Newspaper Filing Manuals." Paper presented at the 54th Annual Conference of the Special Libraries Association, Denver, CO, 9-13 June 1963. (ANPA 63-12)

361. Schaeffer, Rex. "Subject Heading Control." Paper presented at the 71st Annual Conference of the Special Libraries Association, Washington, DC, 7-12 June 1980. (ANPA 80-11)

362. Schaeffer, Rex. "Subject Heading Control for a Newspaper Clipping File." Paper presented at the 62nd Annual Conference of the Special Libraries Association, San Francisco, CA, 6-10 June 1971. (ANPA 71-3)

363. Shoemaker, Ralph J. "Newspaper Library Filing Systems." Paper presented at the 52nd Annual Conference of the Special Libraries Association, San Francisco, CA, May 28 - June 1, 1961. (ANPA 61-3)

364. Shoemaker, Ralph J. *Subject Classifications for Clipping and Picture Files*. New York: American Newspaper Publishers Association, September 1958.

365. Shoemaker, Ralph J. "Weeding and Other Space-Saving Methods." *Special Libraries* 47 (October 1956): 357-360. Paper presented at the 47th Annual Conference of the Special Libraries Association, Pittsburgh, PA, 3-7 June 1956.

366. Sloan, W.J. "*New York Times* Picture Library." *SLA Picture Division Picturescope* 3 (July 1955): 9-10.

367. Slote, Stanley J. "Approach to Weeding Criteria for Newspaper Libraries." *American Documentation* 19 (April 1968): 168-172.

368. Smythe, Eric J.C. "Press Cuttings." *Aslib Proceedings* 1 (August 1949): 105-112.

369. Somers, Lewis S. "What Can the Newspaper Library Do to Conserve Zinc?" *Special Libraries* 34 (July-August 1943): 306-308.

370. Stern, Joan. "Practical Photo Preservation -- A Contradiction in Terms." Paper presented at the 73rd Annual Conference of the Special Libraries Association, Detroit, MI, 5-10 June 1982. (ANPA 82-8)

371. Stout, Ruth. "Weeding." Paper presented at the 64th Annual Conference of the Special Libraries Association, Pittsburgh, PA, 10-14 June 1973. (ANPA 73-9)

372. "Subject Classification Breakdown at the *Chicago Sun-Times*." Paper presented at the 53rd Annual Conference of the Special Libraries Association, Washington, DC, 27-31 May 1962. (ANPA 62-8)

373. "Subject Heading Reports and Discussions." Presented at the 57th Annual Conference of the Special Libraries Association, Minneapolis, MN, May 29 - June 2 1966. (ANPA 66-11)

374. Sullivan, Bernice. "The Filing of Art, Veloxes and Negatives at the *Journal Star* Library, Lincoln, Nebraska." Paper presented at the 67th Annual Conference of the Special Libraries Association, Denver, CO, 6-10 June 1976. (ANPA 76-12)

375. Symonds, Maurice. "Romance of a Picture -- From the Photographer to the Files." *Special Libraries* 27 (March 1936): 69-70.

376. Symonds, Maurice. "War Pictures." *Special Libraries* 31 (July-August 1940): 231-232. Paper presented at the 32nd Annual Conference of the Special Libraries Association, Indianapolis, IN, 3-6 June 1940.

377. Szigethy, Marion. "A Computer Produced Thesaurus for the Clipping File." Paper presented at the 61st Annual Conference of the Special Libraries Association, Detroit, MI, 7-11 June 1970. (ANPA 70-6)

378. "Thesaurus Updated as Librarians Aid." *Editor and Publisher* 102 (April 19, 1969): 82.

379. Thompson, Gayle, and others. *Subject Classification*. Arlington, VA: ERIC Document Reproduction Service, ED 107 273, 1974. Paper presented at the 65th Annual Conference of the Special Libraries Association, Toronto, Canada, 9-13 June 1974.

380. Trivedi, Harish. *An Alternative System of Subject Classification for Media Libraries*. Arlington, VA: ERIC Document Reproduction Service, ED 107 275, 1974. Paper presented at the 65th Annual Conference of the Special Libraries Association, Toronto, Canada, 9-13 June 1974. (ANPA 74-9)

381. Viskochil, Larry A. "What the Future Holds for Newspaper Photo Collections." Paper presented at the 72nd Annual Conference of the Special Libraries Association, Atlanta, GA, 13-18 June 1981. (ANPA 81-14)

382. Vitek, Clement G. "Standardization of Subject Headings in Newspaper Clippings Collections." Paper presented at the 56th Annual Conference of the Special Libraries Association, Philadelphia, PA, 6-10 June 1965. (ANPA 65-13)

383. Webber, Olga. "Trimming the Clipping Files by the 7R's." Special Libraries 60 (February 1969): 82-86. Paper presented at the 59th Annual Conference of the Special Libraries Association, Los Angeles, CA, 2-7 June 1968.

384. Whatmore, Geoffrey. "Classification for News Libraries (with Discussion)." Aslib Proceedings 25 (June 1973): 207-215.

385. Wolf, David. "New Approach to Newspaper Clipping Files." Paper presented at the 57th Annual Conference of the Special Libraries Association, Minneapolis, MN, May 29 - June 2 1966. (ANPA 66-9)

386. Wood, Ellen. "New Copyright Act Changes Rights/Protection for Photos." Editor and Publisher 111 (July 15, 1978): 26.

387. "World of Print: New York Herald Tribune Morgue." Library Journal 92 (December 15, 1967): 4461.

388. Yingling, John. "The New York Times Picture Library." SLA Picture Division Picturescope 3 (July 1955): 10.

389. Zarcone, Beth B. "Time, Inc. Picture Collection." Paper presented at the 75th Annual Conference of the Special Libraries Association, New York, NY 9-14 June 1984. (ANPA 84-14)

REFERENCE MATERIAL IN THE NEWSPAPER LIBRARY

390. Atkinson, Rose Marie. "Government Documents at the U.S. News and World Report." Paper presented at the 75th Annual Conference of the Special Libraries Association, New York, NY, 9-14 June 1984. (ANPA 84-1)

391. Curtiss, Frances E. "Books on the Second World War." Special Libraries 31 (July-August 1940): 232-234. Paper presented at the 44th Annual Conference of the Special Libraries Association, Toronto, Canada, 22-25 June 1953.

392. Johnson, Josephine R. "Newspaper Reference Library: A Suggested List of Basic Books." Special Libraries 62 (April 1971): 174, 176-177.

393. Johnson, Josephine R. "A Suggested List of Reference Books for a Newspaper Reference Library." Paper presented at the 61st Annual Conference of the Special Libraries Association, Detroit, MI, 7-11 June 1970. (ANPA 70-3)

394. McDonald, Lany W. "Commercial Database Survey." Paper presented at the 75th Annual Conference of the Special Libraries Association, New York, NY, 9-14 June 1984. (ANPA 84-6)

395. Ravenna, Lauretta. "Basic Reference Books Suggested for Smaller and Medium-Sized Newspaper Libraries." Paper presented at the 53rd Annual Conference of the Special Libraries Association, Washington, DC, 27-31 May 1962. (ANPA 62-5)

396. Rhydwen, David A. "A List of Reference Books." Paper presented at the 61st Annual Conference of the Special Libraries Association, Detroit, MI, 7-11 June 1970. (ANPA 70-4)

397. Rhydwen, David A. "North of the Border: Basic Books for a Canadian Newspaper Reference Library." Special Libraries 62 (April 1971): 175, 177-78.

398. Shoemaker, Ralph J. "Weeding and Other Space-Saving Methods." Special Libraries 47 (October 1956): 357-360. Paper presented at the 47th Annual Conference of the Special Libraries Association, Pittsburgh, PA, 3-7 June 1956.

399. Smith, Evelyn E. "Newspaper Library Reference Collections." Special Libraries 55 (November 1964): 628-631. Paper presented at the 55th Annual Conference of the Special Libraries Association, St. Louis, MO, 7-11 June 1964. (ANPA 64-11)

400. Trimble, Kathleen. "Government Documents at U.S. News and World Report." Paper presented at the 75th Annual Conference of the Special Libraries Association, New York, NY, 9-14 June 1984. (ANPA 84-12)

401. Wood, Ellen. "Newspaper Library Basics - Reference." Paper presented at the 71st Annual Conference of the Special Libraries Association, Washington, DC, 7-12 June 1980. (ANPA 80-15)

NEWSPAPER INDEXING

402. "*Akron Beacon Journal* Topical Clip Index." Paper presented at the 58th Annual Conference of the Special Libraries Association, New York, NY, May 28 - June 1 1967. (ANPA 67-1)

403. "Albany County Library Begins Newspaper Indexing." *Wyoming Library Roundup* 33 (December 1977): 36-37.

404. Armstrong, Thomas F., and Janice C. Fennell. "Historical and Genealogical Gold Mine: An Index Project for a Small-Town Newspaper." *RQ* 22 (Winter 1982): 140-145.

405. Birnbaum, Louis H. "Tracing a City's History." *New York Times*, 6 September 1936, sec. 9, p. 9.

406. Blinn, Harold E. "Notes and Suggestions: WPA Newspaper Clipping and Indexing Service." *Pacific Historical Review* 6 (September 1937): 284-287.

407. Breneau, Beth. "Local Press Indexing, A Personal Project." Reference Assistance Papers, No. 1. Wayne State University Libraries, July 1974.

408. Bruncken, Herbert. "Indexing and Filming Newspapers." *Library Journal* 63 (March 15, 1938): 211.

409. "*The Canadian News Index*." *Canadian Library Association Feliciter* 12 (March 1967): 32.

410. "*Canadian Newspaper Index* Announced For 1967." *Library Journal* 92 (April 1, 1967): 1408-1409.

411. "Cataloging Historical Newspaper Collections Begins." *Presstime* 4 (Decmeber 1982): 10.

412. Cavanaugh, Bonnie. "Cooperative Newspaper Indexing." *Sourdough* 15 (January 1978): 9.

413. Chase, William D. "The _Flint Journal_ Index - An Independent Project Serving a Newspaper and a Public Library." Paper presented at the 56th Annual Conference of the Special Libraries Association, Philadelphia, PA, 6-10 June 1965. (ANPA 65-1)

414. Cherry, Susan Spaeth. "Yesterday's News for Tomorrow; A Special Update on News Indexes, Indexing and Indexers." _American Libraries_ 10 (November 1979): 588-592. (See also entries for James Rettig and Daniel Suvak.)

415. Coates, Peter Ralph. "The Retrospective Indexing of Two Colonial Newspapers." _The Indexer_ 13 (April 1983): 183-184.

416. Cole, Carol, and Joseph C. Scorza. "The Care and Feeding of a Newspaper Index: A Selected Bibliography." _Unabashed Librarian_ no. 26 (1978): 11-12.

417. Colvin, Gloria Payne. "Bridging the Local Information Gap: A Propasal for Developing an Index to the _Durham Morning Herald_ and the _Durham Sun_." Master's thesis, University of North Carolina, April 1980.

418. Curry, Arthur R. "Newspaper Index in Galveston." _Wilson Bulletin for Librarians_ 9 (May 1935): 504. (Comment on Paul P. Foster's "Neglected Sources of History.")

419. Dewe, Michael. "Indexing Local Newspapers." _The Assistant Librarian_ 65 (April 1972): 58-59.

420. Drummond, Norman. "Current Affairs: A Mitchell Library Viewpoint." _SLA News_ no. 146 (July 1978): 133-135.

421. Eaton, James J. "Newspaper Indexing." In _Proceedings of the 14th Conference_, 42-48. London: Association of Special Libraries and Information Bureaux, 1937. Paper presented at the 29th Annual Conference of the Special Libraries Association, New York, NY, 16-19 June 1937.

422. Einhorn, Judith Meister. _Guidelines for Indexing Local Newspapers_. Westerly, RI: South County Interrelated Library System, 1976.

423. Faulkner, Ronnie W. "dBase III and Newspaper Indexing." *Library Software Review* 4 (September-October 1985): 280-284.

424. Fikes, Robert, Jr. *Newspaper Indexes, Guides, Directories, and Union Lists, No. 4.* Arlington, VA: ERIC Document Reproduction Service, ED 156 152, 1978.

425. Fitch, Maude E. "Newspaper Indexing in San Diego." *Library Journal* 63 (June 15, 1938): 493-495.

426. Foster, Paul P. "Neglected Sources of History." *Wilson Bulletin for Librarians* 9 (March 1935): 351-357. (See also entries for Arthur R. Curry, Mona Harrop, and Alfred Rawlinson.)

427. Foster, Paul P. "Shall We Advocate a News Index?" *Special Libraries* 27 (October 1936): 276-277.

428. Frankland, John. "A Computer Printed Index for Newspaper Libraries." Paper presented at the 60th Annual Conference of the Special Libraries Association, Montreal, Canada, 1-5 June 1969. (ANPA 69-3)

429. Frankland, John. "Milwaukee (WI) Journal Index." Paper presented at the 64th Annual Conference of the Special Libraries Association, 10-14 June 1973. (ANPA 73-2)

430. Friedman, Harry A. *Newspaper Indexing.* Milwaukee, WI: Marquette University Press, 1942.

431. Furth, Stephen E. "Mechanized Information Storage and Retrieval Made Easy." *Special Libraries* 54 (November 1963): 569-571. Paper presented at the 54th Annual Conference of the Special Libraries Association, Denver, CO, 9-13 June 1963. (ANPA 63-6)

432. Galvin, Glenda I. "Index to Diamond Jubilee Issue of *The Leader-Post.*" Master's thesis, Catholic University of America, May 1967.

433. Gephart, Joseph C. "The New York Times Index." *Special Libraries* 49 (December 1958): 482-488.

434. Ghosh, S. "Printed Newspaper Index." *IASLIC Bulletin* 26 no. 2 (1981): 77-82.

435. Gilzinger, Donald, Jr. "Creation of an In-House Newspaper Index." *Community and Junior College Libraries* 2 (Spring 1984): 9-13.

436. Goyal, Sat Paul, and Chhotey Lal. "Newspaper Indexing in India." *Indian Association of Special Libraries and Information Centres Bulletin* 14 (March 1970): 1.

437. Greengrass, Alan R. "Indexing at the New York Times Information Service." In *Indexing Specialized Formats and Subjects*, edited by Hilda Feinberg, 180-188. Metuchen, NJ: Scarecrow Press, Inc., 1983.

438. Griffin, Walter R., and Jay L. Rasmussen, comps. "A Comprehensive Guide to the Location of Published and Unpublished Newspaper Indexes in North Carolina Depositories." *North Carolina Libraries* 32 (Fall 1974): 11-25.

439. Gwinup, Thomas. "Survey of Local Newspapers in California." *California Librarian* 36 (January 1975): 4-10.

440. Hales, David A. "Indexing Alaska's Newspapers." *Sourdough* 18 (January 1981): 9-10.

441. Hales, David A. "Newspaper Indexing: The State of the Art." *Sourdough* 18 (April - June 1981): 18, 25.

442. Hales, David A., and Brenda Artman. "Alaska Newspaper Index: Microcomputers and Information Access Company." *Reference Services Review* 11 (Fall 1983): 48-52.

443. Harris, Margaret. "Alaska Library Association Newspaper Indexing Conference." *Sourdough* 11 (Winter 1974): 18.

444. Harrop, Mona. "Cincinnati's Newspaper Index." (letter) *Wilson Bulletin for Librarians* 9 (May 1935): 504. (Response to Paul P. Foster's article "Neglected Sources of History.")

445. Holmes, Grace. "The London Gazette Index." *The Indexer* 4 (Spring 1964): 13-16.

446. "Hugh Index of News Clippings Finished." *Editor and Publisher* 100 (September 30, 1967): 28.

447. "In Response to a Growing Demand." *Library of Congress Information Bulletin* 28 (November 26, 1969): 644.

448. "Indexes of Florida Newspapers." *Florida Libraries* 20 (June 1969): 87.

449. Irwin, John, and Sally Shook, comps. *Flagstaff Cooperative Newspaper Indexing Project. Manual.* Arlington, VA: ERIC Document Reproduction Service, ED 105 842, 1974.

450. James, Barbara. "Indexing *The Times*." *The Indexer* 11 (October 1979): 209-211.

451. Janda, Kenneth, and David Gordon. "Microfilm Information Retrieval System for Newspaper Libraries." *Special Libraries* 61 (January 1970): 33-47. Paper presented at the 60th Annual Conference of the Special Libraries Association, Montreal, Canada, 1-5 June 1969. (ANPA 69-4)

452. Jennings, Anne B. "Indexing in Small and Medium-Sized Libraries." Paper presented at the 64th Annual Conference of the Special Libraries Association, 10-14 June 1973. (ANPA 73-4)

453. Johnpoll, Bernard K. "Canada News Index: A Report on a Computerized Indexing of News in Selected Canadian Dailies." *Special Libraries* 58 (February 1967): 102-105. Paper presented at the 57th Annual Conference of the Special Libraries Association, Minneapolis, MN, May 29 - June 2 1966.

454. Knee, Michael. "An Evaluation of the UNIVAC 1100/82 Text Editor as an Alternative Word Processor for Generating a Newspaper Index." Information Services and Use 4 (April 1984): 31-36.

455. Knee, Michael. "Producing a Local Newspaper Index." The Indexer 13 (October 1982): 101-103.

456. Koch, Jean E. "Newspaper Indexing: Planning and Options." Special Libraries 76 (Fall 1985): 271-281.

457. Kruse, Rhoda. "Newspaper Indexing." News Notes of California Libraries 72 (1977): 25-29.

458. Kuzel, Judith F. "Specialized Reference Indexes and Their Use By Adults." Illinois Libraries 48 (September 1966): 516-518.

459. Kyte, Colin H.J. "Indexing The Times." Library Association Record 71 (January 1969): 6-9.

460. Kyte, Colin H.J. "The Times Index." Indexer 5 (Spring 1967): 125-129.

461. La Hood, Charles G., Jr. "Newspapers: Directories, Indexes and Union Lists." Library Trends 15 (January 1967): 420-429.

462. Ladenson, Alex. "The Newspaper Index." Library Journal 66 (April 1, 1941): 275.

463. Lathrop, Mary Lou, and Norman M. Lathrop. Lathrop Report on Newspaper Indexes. Wooster, OH: Norman Lathrop Enterprises, 1979.

464. Lathrop, Norman M. "Approach to Newspaper Indexing, Flint Journal Project." RQ 3 (May 1964): 11-12.

465. Lothrop, Jean W. "Indexing the Local Newspaper: An Economical Approach." South Dakota Library Bulletin 55 (October-December 1969): 227-236.

466. Lundy, Karen L. "Update On Kalamazoo Indexing." American Libraries 11 (May 1980): 255.

467. McDermott, Philip Wayne. "WPA Newspaper Indexing Project." Library Occurrent 13 (October-December 1940): 229.

468. Meyers, Pamela. "Newspaper Indexing at Bell and Howell Microphoto." Paper presented at the 71st Annual Conference of the Special Libraries Association, Washington, DC, 7-12 June 1980. (ANPA 80-10)

469. Michael, James J. "To Clip Or Not to Clip That Is the Question." PLA News 16 (Spring 1977): 7-8.

470. Mike, Sister Mary de Paul. "An Analytical, Cumulative Index to The Record (Louisville, KY) for the Years 1950 Through 1960." Master's thesis, Catholic University of America, 1966.

471. Mills, T.F. "Preserving Yesterday's News for Today's Historian: A Brief History of Newspaper Preservation, Bibliography, and Indexing." Journal of Library History 16 (Summer 1981): 463-487.

472. Milner, Anita Cheek. Newspaper Indexes: A Location and Subject Guide for Researchers. Metuchen, NJ: Scarecrow Press, Inc., 1977.

473. Milstead, Jessica L. "Newspaper Indexing: the Official Washington Post Index." In Indexing Specialized Formats and Subjects, edited by Hilda Feinberg, 189-204. Metuchen, NJ: Scarecrow Press, Inc., 1983.

474. Mischo, William H. "Computer-Produced Newspaper Index." Journal of Library Automation 10 (March 1977): 41-52.

475. Newman, John, and Patricia Richter. Indexing Local Newspapers. Technical Leaflet 107. Nashville, TN: American Association for State and Local History, 1978.

476. "Newspaper Index on Microfilm Project." Library Journal 92 (June 1, 1967): 2112.

477. "Newspaper Indexing Center." *Sci-Tech News* 24 (September 1970): 31.

478. "Newspaper Indexing for WPA Projects." *Journal of Documentary Reproduction* 2 (March 1939): 46-47.

479. "Newspaper Indexing Project." *Library News Bulletin* 8 (March 1940): 5.

480. Nomer, Genevieve Trevor. "A Guide to Developing a Computerized Local News Index." Master's thesis, Glassboro State College, 1974.

481. "Notes on Newspaper Indexing." In *Report of Proceedings of the 14th Conference*, 39-41. London: Association of Special Libraries and Information Bureaux, 1937.

482. Oetting, E.C. "Indexing Student Newspapers." *American Archivist* 43 (Spring 1980): 211-212.

483. Pasqua, Tom; Robert Rayfield; and Stuart Showalter. "Automated Indexing for Newspapers: Two Suggested Approaches." *Journalism Quarterly* 52 (Summer 1975): 291-296.

484. Perica, Esther. "A Newspaper Index--Good Sense--Sound Journalism." *School Press Review* 52 (May 1976): 7, 10.

485. Perica, Esther. *Newspaper Indexing for Historical Societies, Colleges, and High Schools*. Monroe, NY: Library Research Associates, 1975.

486. *Plan for a Newspaper Index Project*. Milwaukee Newspaper Index. Milwaukee, WI: WPA, 1941.

487. Quill, Edward. "A Computerized Storage and Retrieval System." Paper presented at the 58th Annual Conference of the Special Libraries Association, New York, NY, May 28 - June 1, 1967. (ANPA 67-4)

488. Rawlinson, Alfred. "A South Carolina Project, Etc." (letter) Wilson Bulletin for Librarians 9 (May 1935): 504-505. (Response to Paul P. Foster's "Neglected Sources of History.")

489. Raye, Sally, and Linda Roberts. "Special Report: Newspaper Indexing -- The Computer Is the Answer." Wilson Library Bulletin 53 (June 1979): 686-687.

490. Reinke, Mary. "The Uses of Newspaper Indices." Tennessee Librarian 4 (May 1952): 5-6.

491. "Response to a Growing Demand: The Newspaper Indexing Center." Library of Congress Information Bulletin 26 (November 26, 1969): 644.

492. Rettig, James. "Costly to Index Local Paper." (letter) American Libraries 11 (February 1980): 86. (Response to Susan Cherry's "Yesterday's News for Tomorrow.")

493. Rhydwen, David A. "Indexing of Negatives Using Kalvar at the Toronto Globe and Mail." Paper presented at the 57th Annual Conference of the Special Libraries Association, Minneapolis, MN, May 29 - June 2 1966. (ANPA 66-6)

494. "San Diego Gets $67,000 to Index Newspaper." Library Journal 92 (September 1, 1967): 2876.

495. San Diego Public Library. Reference Department. Newspaper Indexing. Author, 1938.

496. Sausedo, Ann. "Marketing the Index." Paper presented at the 64th Annual Conference of the Special Libraries Association, 10-14 June 1973. (ANPA 73-6)

497. Schaeffer, Rex. "Punched Card Indexing for Newspaper Libraries." Paper presented at the 55th Annual Conference of the Special Libraries Association, St. Louis, MO, 7-11 June 1964. (ANPA 64-9)

498. "School Develops Index to Local News Stories." *Editor and Publisher* 111 (October 14, 1978): 15.

499. Seeliger, Ronald. "The *Texas Observer* Index, 1954-1970." *Texas Library Journal* 48 (September 1972): 189.

500. Sell, Kenneth D. "A Checklist of Published Indexes to Current American Daily Newspapers." *RQ* 17 (Fall 1977): 13-16.

501. Semonche, Barbara P. "Electronic Newspaper Indexing Using an IBM PC." Paper presented at the 76th Annual Conference of the Special Libraries Association, Winnipeg, Canada, 8-13 June 1985.

502. Shaftesley, John M. "The *Jewish Chronicle* Index, 1841- ." *The Indexer* 4 (Spring 1964): 3-13.

503. Shoemaker, Ralph J. "Newspaper Library Filing Systems." Paper presented at the 52nd Annual Conference of the Special Libraries Association, San Francisco, CA, May 28 - June 1 1961. (ANPA 61-3)

504. Sholtys, Pauline M. "Adapting Library of Congress Subject Headings for Newspaper Indexing." *Cataloging and Classification Quarterly* 4 (Summer 1984): 99-102.

505. Smith, Donald R. *Newspaper Indexing Handbook for Small Libraries*. Arlington, VA: ERIC Document Reproduction Service, ED 191 422, 1978.

506. Stafford, Robert. "Australian Newspaper Index Feasibility Study." Canberra: National Library of Australia, 1980.

507. Stewart, Robert W. "Notes on Some New Jersey Newspaper Indexes." *New Jersey Libraries* New Series 1 (Winter 1968): 5-9.

508. Suvak, Daniel. "Update On News Indexing." (letter) *American Libraries* 11 (January 1980): 16. (Response to Susan Cherry's "Yesterday's News for Tomorrow.")

509. Thaxton, Lyn, and Mary Edith Redus. "Of Migraines and Maddox: The Making of the Atlanta Constitution Index." RQ 14 (Spring 1975): 225-227.

510. Tomlinson, Laurence E. "Indexes to Newspapers." Library Journal 61 (October 1, 1936): 709-710.

511. Ver Hulz, Jack, and Alfred S. Tauber. "Microfilm Information Storage and Retrieval." Paper presented at the 59th Annual Conference of the Special Libraries Association, Los Angeles, CA, 2-7 June 1968. (ANPA 68-1)

512. Vierra, Bobbie, and Tom Trice. "Local Newspaper Indexing: A Public Library Reports Its Experience." Serials Librarian 5 (Fall 1980): 87-92.

513. Vitek, Clement G. "The Advantages of a Newspaper Index." Paper presented at the 53rd Annual Conference of the Special Libraries Association, Washington, DC, 27-31 May 1962. (ANPA 62-9)

514. Vitek, Clement G. "A Philosophy of Newspaper Indexing." Paper presented at the 64th Annual Conference of the Special Libraries Association, Pittsburgh, PA, 10-14 June 1973. (ANPA 73-10)

515. Walker, Marie-Anne E. "Newspaper Indexing in the United States." Association of Special Libraries Proceedings 14 (1937): 31-38. Paper presented at the 29th Annual Conference of the Special Libraries Association, New York, NY, 16-19 June 1937.

516. Wallis, Elizabeth J. "The Changing Times." The Indexer 11 (April 1979): 144.

517. Webber, Olga, and others. "Management of Auxiliary Storage and Retrieval Systems, Including Transcript of Discussion and Talks." Presented at the 59th Annual Conference of the Special Libraries Association, Los Angeles, CA, 2-7 June 1968. (ANPA 68-2)

518. "White Hall Newspaper Index." *Illinois Libraries* 23 (May 1941): 18.

519. Williamson, Wilbert E. *Indexes to Michigan Newspapers*. Reference Assistance Papers No. 3. Wayne State University Libraries, March 1975.

520. Winchell, F. Mabel. "Another Newspaper Indexing Project." (letter) *Wilson Bulletin For Librarians* 9 (June 1935): 589.

521. Zeskey, Russell H. "Newspapers on Microfilm: History As It Was Happening (and Indexes to Help You Find Your Way)." *Serials Librarian* 4 (Summer 1980): 393-399.

MICROFORMS

522. Barensfeld, Tom. "Mysteries of the Rue 'Morgue': Push-Button Library System Set Up for Cleveland Press." Scripps-Howard News (August 1969): 3-6.

523. Bruncken, Herbert. "Indexing and Filming Newspapers." Library Journal 63 (March 15, 1938): 211.

524. Burell, Perry, Jr. "New Innovations in Microfilm." Paper presented at the 62nd Annual Conference of the Special Libraries Association, San Francisco, CA, 6-10 June 1971. (ANPA 71-1)

525. Chapman, Ronald F., and Takumi Tashima. "Preserving Hawaii's History: Microfilming the Predecessors of the Honolulu Star-Bulletin." Hawaii Library Association Journal 31 (December 1974): 30-32.

526. Doncevic, Lois A. "Automated Microfilm Systems in Small Libraries." Paper presented at the 73rd Annual Conference of the Special Libraries Association, Detroit, MI, 5-10 June 1982. (ANPA 82-1)

527. Doncevic, Lois A. "Electronic Libraries." ANPA Research Institute R.I. Bulletin no. 1336 (October 10, 1979): 401-402.

528. "Dual Film Cards Cut Morgue Space in News Library." Editor and Publisher 100 (January 28, 1967): 48.

529. "Elke Exposure Control System for Microfilming Newspapers and Rare Documents." MICRODOC 17 (1978): 72-73.

530. Fournier, Jacques, and Alison Schoenfeld. "The Development of An Electronic Film Retrieval System for a Newspaper Library." In Proceedings of the American Society for Information Science, v. 10, 36th Annual Meeting, Los Angeles, CA, 21-25 October 1973. Edited by Helen J. Waldron and F. Raymond Long, 67-69. Westport, CT: Greenwood Press, 1973.

531. Harrison, Alice W. "Conservation of Library Materials: Clip No. 11: Newspaper Clipping Files." <u>Atlantic Provinces Library Association Bulletin</u> 43 (September 1979): 6.

532. Haswell, Martha Mullen, and Barbara P. Semonche. <u>Microfilming Newspaper Clippings</u>. Durham, NC: Durham Herald Company, June 1982.

533. Henebry, Agnes C. "Preservation of Photographs on Microfilm: An Experiment." <u>Special Libraries</u> 47 (December 1956): 451-454.

534. Hermann, William H. "Microphotographing Bound Milwaukee Newspapers." <u>Journal of Documentary Reproduction</u> (March 1939): 11-20.

535. Hutton, R.S. "Micro-Photographic Processes in Documentation." <u>Report of Proceedings of the 14th Aslib Conference</u> (1937): 96-99.

536. Ippolito, Andrew V. "What's New in Equipment?" Paper presented at the 63rd Annual Conference of the Special Libraries Association, Boston, MA, 4-8 June 1972. (ANPA 72-1)

537. Janda, Kenneth, and David Gordon. "Microfilm Information Retrieval System for Newspaper Libraries." <u>Special Libraries</u> 61 (January 1970): 33-47. Paper presented at the 60th Annual Conference of the Special Libraries Association, Montreal, Canada, 1-5 June 1969. (ANPA 69-4)

538. King, Roy T. "The Microfilm Project of the <u>St. Louis Post-Dispatch</u>." Paper presented at the 60th Annual Conference of the Special Libraries Association, Montreal, Canada, 1-5 June 1969. (ANPA 69-5)

539. McArthur, D.W. "Interface of Computer with Microfilm." Paper presented at the 60th Annual Conference of the Special Libraries Association, Montreal, Canada, 1-5 June 1969. (ANPA 69-6)

540. Majumdar, Gopal Kumar. *Newspaper Microfilming: A Plea for Newsprint Documentation*. Calcutta: Firma K.L. Mukhopadhyay, 1974.

541. "Microfilm Aids Readers of Ohio Newspaper." *Editor and Publisher* 110 (June 11, 1977): 20, 40.

542. Miller, Diane. "Pantagraph Microfiche System." Paper presented at the 73rd Annual Conference of the Special Libraries Association, Detroit, MI, 5-10 June 1982. (ANPA 82-7)

543. Mills, T.F. "Preserving Yesterday's News for Today's Historian: A Brief History of Newspaper Preservation, Bibliography, and Indexing." *Journal of Library History* 16 (Summer 1981): 463-487.

544. Mooney, Shirley E. "Microfilm Vs. Database." *Production News* 5 (September 1980): 30, 60.

545. Oppedahl, Alison; Leon Bloom; Jim Criswell; and Janice Lewis. *Will Microfilm and Computers Replace Clippings?* Arlington, VA: ERIC Document Reproduction Service, ED 107 274, June 1974. Paper presented at the 65th Annual Conference of the Special Libraries Association, Toronto, Canada, 9-13 June 1974. (ANPA 74-5)

546. Power, Eugene B. "The Use of Sheet Film for Newspaper Clippings." *Special Libraries* 45 (March 1954): 111-114. Paper presented at the 44th Annual Conference of the Special Libraries Association, Toronto, Canada, 22-25 June 1953.

547. Rhydwen, David A. "The Application of Microphotography to Newspaper Clippings." *Special Libraries* 55 (January 1964): 28-30. Paper presented at the 54th Annual Conference of the Special Libraries Association, Denver, CO, 9-13 June 1963. (ANPA 63-10)

548. Rhydwen, David A. "Indexing of Negatives Using Kalvar at the Toronto *Globe and Mail*." Paper presented at the 57th Annual Conference of the Special Libraries Association, Minneapolis, MN, May 29 - June 2, 1966. (ANPA 66-6)

549. Rhydwen, David A. "Microfilm and a Newspaper Clipping File." *Journal of Micrographics* 1 no. 1 (1967): 8-11.

550. Rhydwen, David A. "Microfilming of Clippings Using Kalvar Microfiche." Paper presented at the 57th Annual Conference of the Special Libraries Association, Minneapolis, MN, May 29 - June 2 1966. (ANPA 66-7)

551. Rhydwen, David A. "Planning a Microfilm Program." Paper presented at the 63rd Annual Conference of the Special Libraries Association, Boston, MA, 4-8 June 1972. (ANPA 72-5)

552. Riker, Elaine M. "Microfilming Newspaper Clippings." *Special Libraries* 56 (November 1965): 655-656. Paper presented at the 56th Annual Conference of the Special Libraries Association, Philadelphia, PA, 6-10 June 1965. (ANPA 65-9)

553. Rogers, David G. "Microfilm Development; Abridged." *Special Libraries* 31 (July-August 1940): 235-237.

554. "San Francisco Examiner Reduces 500 Filing Cabinets to 12 Via Bell and Howell Microfilm System." *Production News* (February 1981): 24-26.

555. Sandt, Roger W. "Micro-Publishing at the *Wall Street Journal*." In *Proceedings of the American Society for Information Science, Annual Meeting*, v. 6, 329-331. Westport, CT: Greenwood Publishing Corp., 1969.

556. Schmidt, Richard. "Does Microfilm Hold Up?" Paper presented at the 61st Annual Conference of the Special Libraries Association, Detroit, MI, 7-11 June 1970. (ANPA 70-5)

557. Schmidt, Richard. "New Innovations in Microfilm." Paper presented at the 62nd Annual Conference of the Special Libraries Association, San Francisco, CA, 6-10 June 1971. (ANPA 71-4)

558. Schoenfeld, Alison. "Miracode for a Newspaper Library." Paper presented at the 63rd Annual Conference of the Special Libraries Association, Boston, MA, 4-8 June 1972. (ANPA 72-6)

559. Spiers, David. "New Innovations in Microfilm." Paper presented at the 62nd Annual Conference of the Special Libraries Association, San Francisco, CA, 6-10 June 1971. (ANPA 71-5)

560. Stack, John P. "Computer Assisted Microfilm Retrieval at the Daily Mirror." Reprographics Quarterly 15 (Autumn 1982): 146-148.

561. Vance, Julia M. "Micrographics in News Libraries." Paper presented at the 71st Annual Conference of the Special Libraries Association, Washington, DC, 7-12 June 1980. (ANPA 80-14)

562. Ver Hulz, Jack, and Alfred S. Tauber. "Microfilm Information Storage and Retrieval." Paper presented at the 59th Annual Conference of the Special Libraries Association, Los Angeles, CA, 2-7 June 1968. (ANPA 68-1).

563. Whatmore, Geoffrey; John Daligan; and Tony Archard. "A Microfilm System for Press Cuttings." Reprographics Quarterly 10 (April 1977): 49-51.

AUTOMATION AND THE NEWSPAPER LIBRARY

564. "The ANPA Advanced Research Program at M.I.T." ANPA Research Institute *R.I. Bulletin* no. 977 (December 27, 1968): 453-460.

565. ANPA. "Library School Courses on Computers in the United States and Canada." Paper presented at the 61st Annual Conference of the Special Libraries Association, Detroit, MI, 7-11 June 1970. (ANPA 70-1)

566. "Advanced Software Systems Designed for Data Capture." *Editor and Publisher* 107 (June 15, 1974): 36, 72.

567. Ahnen, Pearl. "Detroit *Free Press* Ready for Electronic Retrieval." *Editor and Publisher* 114 (October 24, 1981): 58, 60.

568. "All the News That's Fit to Retrieve (Computerized Retrieval Service Providing Access to World News)." *Wilson Library Bulletin* 54 (November 1979): 152.

569. Andrews, Elliott E. "This Works for Us . . . Staff Organization." *Special Libraries* 54 (March 1963): 162. Abstracted from paper presented at the 53rd Annual Conference of the Special Libraries Association, Washington, DC, 27-31 May 1962. (ANPA 62-1)

570. Ashe, Reid. "Electronic Publishing." Paper presented at the 72nd Annual Conference of the Special Libraries Association, Atlanta, GA, 13-18 June 1981. (ANPA 81-1)

571. "Automated Information Bank Services Come to CRS (Congressional Research Services)." *Library of Congress Information Bulletin* 32 (September 7, 1973): 313.

572. "Automated News Clipping, Indexing, and Retrieval System (ANCIRS)." *Journal of Library Automation* 7 (September 1974): 235.

573. "Automated System: File Drawer Comes to Clerk in Library." *Editor and Publisher* 100 (August 5, 1967): 15, 43.

574. Bachelder, Sally. "The *New York Times* Information Bank: A User's Perspective." In *The Use of Computers in Literature Searching and Related Reference Activities in Libraries*, edited by F. Wilfred Lancaster. Urbana-Champaign, IL: University of Illinois, 1976.

575. Bachelder, Sally. Letter. *RQ* 16 (Spring 1977): 264. (Comments on Rhoda Garoogian's article, "Library Use of New York Times Information Bank.")

576. Baird, Kathleen Hunt. "Computerized Libraries and Newsrooms." *Presstime* 1 (December 1979): 28.

577. Bant, Geoffery, and Dennis Dearnbarger. "Automated Library Makes File Referencing Easy." *Spectrum* 4 (Spring 1985): 20-21.

578. Barensfeld, Tom. "Q & A: There's Still No Computer Code to Rival Newspaper Librarian." *Scripps-Howard News* (August 1980): 3.

579. *Basic Specifications for a Full-Text On-Line Automated Newspaper Library System*. Newspaper Division, Special Libraries Association, 1980.

580. Batliner, Doris. "Our Lovable Idiot (Computerized Library Retrieval System)." Paper presented at the 71st Annual Conference of the Special Libraries Association, Washington, DC, 7-12 June 1980. (ANPA 80-1)

581. Batliner, Doris. "XM Retrieval System -- Fact Sheet." Paper presented at the 67th Annual Conference of the Special Libraries Association, Denver, CO, 6-10 June 1976. (ANPA 76-1)

582. "Battelle, DEC Offer Private File Start-Up Service for Newspaper Libraries." *Online Database Review* 4 (May 1983): 9.

583. Billings, Thomas N. "Electronic Morgue Deferred by Information Retrieval Problems." Newspaper Controller 21 (April 1967): 2-3, 9.

584. Borkowski, Casimir. "An Experimental System for Automated Indexing for Personal Names and Personal Titles in Newspaper Texts." American Documentation 18 (July 1967): 131-138.

585. "Boston Globe and NYTIS Begin New Regional Newspaper Database." Online 5 (July 1981): 60-61.

586. "Boston Globe Renovation Reduces VDT Glare." Editor and Publisher 113 (June 7, 1980): 60, 70.

587. "Breakthrough Achieved with $7500 Electronic Library Programs." Editor and Publisher 114 (September 19, 1981): 28, 31.

588. Cappiello, Alex. "Ragen MRS-90 Graphic Communication System." Paper presented at the 65th Annual Conference of the Special Libraries Association, Toronto, Canada, 9-13 June 1974. (ANPA 74-1)

589. "Cataloging Historical Newspaper Collections Begins." Presstime 4 (December 1982): 10.

590. Catanese, Peter J. "Electronic Newspaper Libraries; Using Mead Corporation's Data/Central Information Storage and Retrieval System." Paper presented at the 67th Annual Conference of the Special Libraries Association, Denver, CO, 6-10 June 1976. (ANPA 76-3)

591. Chao, Jennifer. "Automation of News Clipping Collections." Paper presented at the 71st Annual Conference of the Special Libraries Association, Washington, DC, 7-12 June 1980. (ANPA 80-2)

592. Chao, Jennifer. "Text Selection." Paper presented at the 72nd Annual Conference of the Special Libraries Association, Atlanta, GA, 13-18 June 1981. (ANPA 81-2)

593. "Clips on Computer Make Retrieval Work a Snap." Editor and Publisher 109 (June 26, 1976): 13.

594. Collins, George M. "Boston Globe Library Computerization Needs (Excerpt of Report)." Paper presented at the 67th Annual Conference of the Special Libraries Association, Denver, CO, 6-10 June 1976. (ANPA 76-4)

595. Collins, George M. "Newspaper Library Automation Update (Mead Systems)." Paper presented at the 68th Annual Conference of the Special Libraries Association, New York, NY, 5-9 June 1977. (ANPA 77-3)

596. "Composing Room Computer Directs Reporters to Old News Stories." Editor and Publisher 107 (April 20, 1974): 96.

597. Corcoran, Maureen. "Mead Data Central and All the News That's Fit to Print." Online 7 (July 1983): 32-35.

598. Crabb, Margaret S. "Library Automation." (letter) Editor and Publisher 100 (September 2, 1967): 7.

599. Criner, Kathleen. "U.S. Government and Teletext: Social and Policy Implications." Paper presented at the 70th Annual Conference of the Special Libraries Association, Honolulu, HI, 9-14 June 1979. (ANPA 79-1)

600. "DEC/Battelle to Provide Full-Text On-Line Library Retrieval System." Editor and Publisher 114 (June 6, 1981): 16, 38.

601. Davis, Charles H.; W. Robert Kearney; and Bonnie M. Davis. "A Computer-Based Procedure for Key-Word Indexing of Newspapers." Journal of the American Society for Information Science 22 (September-October 1971): 348-351.

602. "Demands of Newspaper Librarianship: Specifications for an Optimal Automated Library System." The Indexer 11 (October 1978): 112. Reprinted from U.K. Press Gazette, 12 June 1978.

603. "DOCU/MASTER System Points to Libraries." *Editor and Publisher* 113 (June 7, 1980): 74.

604. Dodge, John. "Technical Problems Put Paper's Morgue on Ice." *MIS Week* 1 (July 2, 1980): 1, 18.

605. Doebler, Paul. "*New York Times* Opens Its Information Bank to Commercial Clients." *Publisher's Weekly* 203 (June 18, 1973): 60-61.

606. Doncevic, Lois A. "Automated Microfilm Systems in Small Libraries." Paper presented at the 73rd Annual Conference of the Special Libraries Association, Detroit, MI, 5-10 June 1982. (ANPA 82-1)

607. Doncevic, Lois A. "Electronic Libraries." ANPA Research Institute *R.I. Bulletin* no. 1336 (October 10, 1979): 401-402.

608. "Do's and Don'ts in Planning an Electronic Library." *Presstime* 4 (December 1982): 10.

609. Duncan, E.E. "Microfiche Collections for the *New York Times* Information Bank." *Microform Review* 2 (October 1973): 269-271.

610. "Electronic Library Systems: Aim Is to Put the Morgue On-Line." *Editor and Publisher* 116 (July 2, 1983): 24, 28.

611. Epstein, Hank. "Introduction to Newspaper Full Text Retrieval Systems." Paper presented at the 72nd Annual Conference of the Special Libraries Association, Atlanta, GA, 13-18 June 1981. (ANPA 81-3)

612. Farquhar, Bob. "The New On-Line News Library in Oklahoma City." Paper presented at the 74th Annual Conference of the Special Libraries Association, New Orleans, LA, 4-9 June 1983. (ANPA 83-1)

613. Farquhar, Bob. "Newspaper Library Goes Online." *Journal of Information and Image Management* 16 (December 1983): 20-21.

614. "First Times Index Comes Off the Computer." Publisher's Weekly 196 (August 18, 1969): 34.

615. Forbes, Harold M. "The West Virginia Newspaper Project." West Virginia Libraries 38 (Winter 1985): 23-24.

616. Fournier, Jacques, and Alison Schoenfeld. "The Development of an Electronic Film Retrieval System for a Newspaper Library." In Proceedings of the American Society for Information Science, vol. 10, 36th Annual Meeting, Los Angeles, CA, 21-25 October 1973. Edited by Helen J. Waldron and F. Raymond Long, 67-69. Westport, CT: Greenwood Press, 1973.

617. Frankland, John. "A Computer Printed Index for Newspaper Libraries." Paper presented at the 60th Annual Conference of the Special Libraries Association, Montreal, Canada, 1-5 June 1969. (ANPA 69-3)

618. Furth, Stephen E. "Mechanized Information Storage and Retrieval Made Easy." Special Libraries 54 (November 1963): 569-571. Paper presented at the 54th Annual Conference of the Special Libraries Association, Denver, CO, 9-13 June 1963. (ANPA 63-6)

619. Gardner, W. David. "All the News That Fits on Fiche." Datamation 18 (November 1972): 169, 172.

620. Garoogian, Rhoda. "Library Use of the New York Times Information Bank: A Preliminary Survey." RQ 16 (Fall 1976): 59-64. (See also entry for Sally Bachelder.)

621. Garrison, Bruce. Computerization of the Newspaper in the 1980's. Arlington, VA: ERIC Document Reproduction Service, ED 234 392, August 1983. Paper presented at the 66th Annual Conference of the Association for Education in Journalism and Mass Communication, Corvallis, GA, 6-9 August 1983.

622. Gloede, Bill. "Electronic Library Systems: Aim Is to Put the Morgue On-Line." Editor and Publisher 116 (July 2, 1983): 24, 28.

623. Greengrass, Alan R. "The Information Bank Thesaurus." ASIS Proceedings of the Conference 15 (1978): 137-140.

624. Greengrass, Alan R. "Information Center Profile: The New York Times Information Bank." Information 6 (January 1974): 29-30.

625. "The Guardian Leads Fleet Street into Electronic Publishing." Online Review 8 (December 1984): 519.

626. Handy, Mary Jane. "Library Automation." Paper presented at the 76th Annual Conference of the Special Libraries Association, Winnipeg, Canada, 8-13 June 1985. (ANPA)

627. "Harnessing the Laser for Newspapers." Newspaper Production (April 1973): 43.

628. Haughey, David. "The News Library: A Key to Future Market Dominance." Editor and Publisher 116 (June 25, 1983): 33-34. (Paper presented at the 74th Annual Conference of the Special Libraries Association, New Orleans, LA, 4-9 June 1983. (ANPA 83-2)

629. Hayes, E. Kenneth. "Newspaper Library Automation Update (Zytron Data Systems)." Paper presented at the 68th Annual Conference of the Special Libraries Association, New York, NY, 5-9 June 1977. (ANPA 77-5)

630. Healey, Gerald B. "News Librarians Rustle Up Electronic Action." Editor and Publisher 108 (June 21, 1975): 29.

631. "Here's How Computerized Library Systems Operate." Presstime 4 (December 1982): 8.

632. Hill, Joy, and others. Photo Storage and Retrieval. Arlington, VA: ERIC Document Reproduction Service, ED 107 278, June 1973. Paper presented at the 64th Annual Conference of the Special Libraries Association, Pittsburgh, PA, 10-14 June 1973. (ANPA 73-3)

633. Hogan, Thomas H. "News Retrieval Services - Growing But Where Are They Headed?" Online Review 3 (September 1979): 247-252.

634. "Information Bank Nearly Ready to Go." Editor and Publisher 104 (July 31, 1971): 37.

635. "Information Bank Picture Story." Online 4 (July 1980): 49-54.

636. "Information Bank II." Wilson Library Bulletin 55 (January 1981): 329.

637. Ippolito, Andrew V. "Automation Committee Report." Paper presented at the 68th Annual Conference of the Special Libraries Association, New York, NY, 5-9 June 1977. (ANPA 77-6)

638. Ippolito, Andrew V. "Databases in Newspaper Libraries." Editor and Publisher 118 (May 11, 1985): 60e-62e.

639. Ippolito, Andrew V. "News Libraries and Automation." Paper presented at the 75th Annual Conference of the Special Libraries Association, New York, NY, 9-14 June 1984. (ANPA 84-3)

640. Jackson, Miles M. "Emerging Information Technologies and the Implications for Special Librarians." Paper presented at the 70th Annual Conference of the Special Libraries Association, Honolulu, HI, 9-14 June 1979. (ANPA 79-4)

641. Janda, Kenneth, and David Gordon. "Microfilm Information Retrieval System for Newspaper Libraries." Special Libraries 61 (January 1970): 33-47. Paper presented at the 60th Annual Conference of the Special Libraries Association, Montreal, Canada, 1-5 June 1969. (ANPA 69-4)

642. Johnpoll, Bernard K. "Canada News Index: A Report on a Computerized Indexing of News in Selected Canadian Dailies." *Special Libraries* 58 (February 1967): 102-105. Paper presented at the 57th Annual Conference of the Special Libraries Association, Minneapolis, MN, May 29-June 2, 1966. (ANPA 66-5)

643. Kabaker, Ray. "Colossus -- A New Technology Enters the Library Automation Update." Paper presented at the 76th Annual Conference of the Special Libraries Association, Winnipeg, Canada, 8-13 June 1985.

644. Kapecky, Michele Ann. "Talking a Good Game (Computer Terminology)." Paper presented at the 71st Annual Conference of the Special Libraries Association, Washington, DC, 7-12 June 1980. (ANPA 80-4)

645. Kapecky, Michele Ann. "Terminology for Computer Novices or Just What *Is* a Mainframe?" Paper presented at the 72nd Annual Conference of the Special Libraries Association, Atlanta, GA, 13-18 June 1981. (ANPA 81-5)

646. Kehl, William B., and J. Francis Reintjes. "Direction and Progress of the Newspaper Research Project at M.I.T." ANPA Research Institute *R.I. Bulletin* no. 936 (November 16, 1967): 307-315.

647. Kesselman, Martin. "Data Base-ics and Trends: The Future of the *New York Times* Online." *Reference Services Review* 11 (Fall 1983): 46-47.

648. "Knight-Ridder Plans Regional Electronic Libraries." *Presstime* 3 (August 1981): 39.

649. Knudson, Donald R., and Richard S. Marcus. "The Design of Microimage Storage and Transmission Capabilities into an Integrated Information Transfer System." *Journal of Micrographics* 6 (September 1972): 15-20.

650. Krayeski, Felix. "The Congressional Research Service Text Processing System." Paper presented at the 71st Annual Conference of the Special Libraries Association, Washington, DC, 7-12 June 1980. (ANPA 80-5)

651. Lage, Sondra B., and Richard S. Marcus. *A Cataloging Manual for a News Retrieval System*. MIT Report ESL-TM-349. Cambridge, MA: Massachusetts Institute of Technology, May 1968.

652. Lancaster, Frederick Wilfrid. "Some Notes on the Possible Effect of Online Information Retrieval Systems on Reporters." Paper presented at the 69th Annual Conference of the Special Libraries Association, Kansas City, MO, 10-15 June 1978. (ANPA 78-2)

653. Lathrop, Norman M. "Approach to Newspaper Indexing, *Flint Journal* Project." *RQ* 3 (May 1964): 11-12.

654. Lee, Leonard S. "Secrets of Successful Systems Design." Paper presented at the 69th Annual Conference of the Special Libraries Association, Kansas City, MO, 10-15 June 1978. (ANPA 78-3)

655. Leigh-Bell, Peter. "BASIL System Uses Automatic Indexing." *Editor and Publisher* 110 (September 10, 1977): 39-40.

656. "Librarian's List of Publications about Computers." *Editor and Publisher* 100 (August 5, 1967): 43.

657. "Librarians Study Automated Systems." *Editor and Publisher* 100 (February 25, 1967): 22.

658. "Library Retrieval System Selected by Kentucky Daily." *Editor and Publisher* 112 (March 10, 1979): 38.

659. Long, John C. "Info-Ky Retrieval System Combines Mini/Microfiche." *Editor and Publisher* 111 (June 3, 1978): 18.

660. McArthur, D.W. "Interface of Computer with Microfilm." Paper presented at the 60th Annual Conference of the Special Libraries Association, Montreal, Canada, 1-5 June 1969. (ANPA 69-6)

661. McCleary, Hunter. "VU/TEXT: Full-Text Daily Newspaper Information . . . and More." *Online* 9 (July 1985): 87-94.

662. McConnell, Robert. "Marketing a News Library Database." Paper presented at the 76th Annual Conference of the Special Libraries Association, Winnipeg, Canada, 8-13 June 1985.

663. McDonald, Lany W. "Commercial Database Survey." Paper presented at the 75th Annual Conference of the Special Libraries Association, New York, NY, 9-14 June 1984. (ANPA 84-6)

664. "Major New Reference Aid Due from New York Times." Publishers Weekly 191 (May 1, 1967): 43-44.

665. Marble, Carol. "On-Line News Information Systems." Canadian Journal of Information Science 4 (May 1979): 79-85.

666. Martin, Homer E., Jr. "How Newspaper Librarians Use Committees to Bring About Change." Paper presented at the 72nd Annual Conference of the Special Libraries Association, Atlanta, GA, 13-18 June 1981. (ANPA 81-6)

667. Martin, Homer E., Jr. "News/Editorial Systems Update." Paper presented at the 71st Annual Conference of the Special Libraries Association, Washington, DC, 7-12 June 1980. (ANPA 80-7)

668. Martin, Homer E., Jr. "News Library Automation Update." Paper presented at the 76th Annual Conference of the Special Libraries Association, Winnipeg, Canada, 8-13 June 1985. (ANPA)

669. Martin, Homer E., Jr. "Newspaper Library Systems: A Comparison." Paper presented at the 75th Annual Conference of the Special Libraries Association, New York, NY, 9-14 June 1984. (ANPA 84-7)

670. May, Barbara. "Dallas Morning News Library Online Authority File." Paper presented at the 71st Annual Conference of the Special Libraries Association, Washington, DC, 7-12 June 1980. (ANPA 80-8)

671. "Mead Data Central Begins Offering New York Times Database Online." Editor and Publisher 116 (April 23, 1983): 97.

672. "Mead Data Distribution of NYTIS Databases Causes Concern and Consternation Among Searching Community . . . Raises Their Ire." *Online* 7 (July 1983): 19-20.

673. Medley, Nora. "Use of the Computer for Subject Heading List." Paper presented at the 71st Annual Conference of the Special Libraries Association, Washington, DC, 7-12 June 1980. (ANPA 80-9)

674. Mest, Elizabeth. "Readers Want More Than Front-Page Stories." *Editor and Publisher* 111 (July 15, 1978): 17-18.

675. Michael, James J. "To Clip or Not to Clip - That Is the Question." *PLA News* 16 (Spring 1977): 7-8.

676. Miller, Tim. "Developing a Database." *Editor and Publisher* 116 (November 12, 1983): 50-51, 53.

677. Miller, Tim. "Fast-Growing Data Base: Knight-Ridder's VU/Text to Provide Electronic Access to Text of AP Newswires and 7 Tribune Co. Papers." *Editor and Publisher* 117 (July 7, 1984): 25-26.

678. Miller, Tim. "Newspapers and Compact Disks." *Editor and Publisher* 118 (November 30, 1985): 22-23.

679. Mischo, William H. "Computer-Produced Newspaper Index." *Journal of Library Automation* 10 (March 1977): 41-52. (Letter by W.C. Crawford - *Journal of Library Automation* 10 (June 1977): 136).

680. Montague, P. McC. "Technological Changes That May Affect Newspaper Libraries in the Future." *Aslib Proceedings* 25 (June 1973): 216-219. Paper presented at a one-day Aslib conference on "The Origins of Modern Newspaper Libraries," London, 23 March 1973.

681. Mooney, Shirley E. "Microfilm vs. Database." *Production News* 5 (September 1980): 30, 60.

682. "Morgue Retrieval System Has Million Page Capacity." *Editor and Publisher* 107 (June 15, 1974); 22, 32.

683. "NEH Funds American Newspaper Databank." *Wilson Library Bulletin* 57 (November 1982): 202.

684. Nash, Mary M. "The *Globe and Mail* Database - A Canadian First." *Online Review* 3 (December 1979): 367-371.

685. "New Canadian News Database Announced." *Online Review* 6 (June 1982): 280.

686. "New Local Newspaper Databases." *Online Review* 7 (April 1983): 87.

687. "*New York Times* Closes Down the Information Bank . . . Licenses Mead Data Central to Distribute NYT Data Bases." *Online* 7 (May 1983): 13.

688. "*N.Y. Times* Index to Be Computerized." *Library Journal* 93 (January 1, 1968): 26.

689. "*New York Times* Index to Go on Computer." *Publishers Weekly* 193 (January 8, 1968): 46-47.

690. "*N.Y. Times* Information Bank to Provide Index Abstracts." *Library Journal* 94 (May 1, 1969): 1831.

691. Newcombe, Barbara, and Harish Trivedi. "Newspapers and Electronic Databases: Present Technology." *Wilson Library Bulletin* 59 (October 1984): 94-97.

692. "News Data Bases: Read All About It." *Canadian Business* 58 (March 1985): 135, 137-138.

693. "News Librarians Don't See Automation in Their Cards." *Editor and Publisher* 96 (September 7, 1963): 15.

694. "Newspaper Articles Easily Retrievable Online." *Keynote* 2 (February 1981): 1. Publication of the Kentucky Department of Libraries and Archives.

695. "Newspaper Librarians to Study Automated System Criteria." *Editor and Publisher* 111 (May 20, 1978): 24.

696. "Newspapers Face Choice in Automating Libraries." *Presstime* 2 (July 1980): 15.

697. "Newsroom Will Be Initial Client: *New York Times* Develops Public Information Bank." *Editor and Publisher* 102 (April 5, 1969): 9, 46.

698. "NEXIS to Include Full Text Business Stories." *SOASIS On the Move* 3 (May 1981): 5.

699. Nomer, Genevieve Trevor. "A Guide to Developing a Computerized Local News Index." Master's thesis, Glassboro, N.J.: Glassboro State College, 1974.

700. "Oklahoma Newspapers Tout Database Service." *Editor and Publisher* 117 (June 2, 1984): 31.

701. Oppedahl, Alison. "Can a Library Become a Profit Center?" *Editor and Publisher* 110 (May 7, 1977): 28.

702. Oppedahl, Alison; Jim Criswell; Leon Bloom; and Janice Lewis. "Will Microfilm and Computers Replace Clippings?" Paper presented at the 65th Annual Conference of the Special Libraries Association, Toronto, Canada, 9-13 June 1974. (ANPA 74-5)

703. "PDP 11/34 Electronic Library System May Also Offset Future AT&T Threat." *Editor and Publisher* 114 (March 14, 1981): 31.

704. "PNI Papers Installing NewsMedia System." *Editor and Publisher* 111 (June 3, 1978): 19.

705. Pasqua, Tom; Robert Rayfield; and Stuart Showalter. "Automated Indexing for Newspapers: Two Suggested Approaches." Journalism Quarterly 52 (Summer 1975): 291-296.

706. Pemberton, J.K. "A Backward and Forward Look at the New York Times Information Bank -- A Tale of Ironies Compounded . . . and an Analysis of the Mead Deal." Online 7 (July 1983): 7-17.

707. Perez, Ernest R. "Electronic Approaches." Editor and Publisher 113 (January 12, 1980): 17-18, 22.

708. Perez, Ernest R. "Newspaper Libraries -- Automated and Non-Automated Systems: Non-Automated Approaches." Editor and Publisher 113 (January 12, 1980): 17-18, 22.

709. Perez, Ernest R. "Text Enhancement: Controlled Vocabulary vs. Free Text." Special Libraries 73 (July 1982): 183-192. Paper presented at the 72nd Annual Conference of the Special Libraries Association, Atlanta, GA, 13-18 June 1981. (ANPA 81-8)

710. Perez, Ernest R. "Text Selection at the Chicago Sun-Times." Paper presented at the 72nd Annual Conference of the Special Libraries Association, Atlanta, GA, 13-18 June 1981. (ANPA 81-7)

711. Perez, Ernest R.; Rex Schaeffer; and Joy Walker. "Subject Heading List Using Linedex, Computer Print-Outs, Index Cards and Computer Access." Paper presented at the 64th Annual Conference of the Special Libraries Association, Pittsburgh, PA, 10-14 June 1973. (ANPA 73-5)

712. "Pitt U, New York Times Have Computer Info Link." Library Journal 98 (January 1, 1973): 14-15.

713. Polansky, Robert B., and Richard S. Marcus. "An Online Computerized News Collector and Selector (Interim Report)." (MIT Report ESL-IR-434) Cambridge, MA: Massachusetts Institute of Technology, 1970.

714. "A Potentially Hugh Database Operation Takes Shape as Mead Technology Readies Network Access to Newspaper and Magazine Files." *Database* 1 (September 1978): 7-8, 68-69.

715. *Preparing for Library Automation*. Bedford, MA: Atex Inc., 1981.

716. Provenzano, Domenic. "NEXIS." *Database* 4 (December 1981): 30-41.

717. Quill, Edward. "A Computerized Storage and Retrieval System." Paper presented at the 58th Annual Conference of the Special Libraries Association, New York, NY, May 28 - June 1 1967. (ANPA 67-4)

718. Quint, Barbara. "Newsbank and News Data Bases." In *Online Search Strategies*, edited by Ryan E. Hoover, 279-304. White Plains, NY: Knowledge Industry Publications, Inc., 1982.

719. Radolf, Andrew. "Electronic Library Service: Automated Libraries are Rapidly Expanding at Newspapers." *Editor and Publisher* 117 (June 30, 1984): 28.

720. Raye, Sally, and Linda Roberts. "Special Report: Newspaper Indexing -- the Computer Is the Answer." *Wilson Library Bulletin* 53 (June 1979): 686-687.

721. Reintjes, J. Francis. "Automatic Indexing for a Computer-Based News Retrieval System." Paper presented at the 63rd Annual Conference of the Special Libraries Association, Boston, MA, 4-8 June 1972. (ANPA 72-4)

722. Reintjes, J. Francis. "Libraries of the Future." Paper presented at the 58th Annual Conference of the Special Libraries Association, New York, NY, May 28-June 1 1967. (ANPA 67-5)

723. Reintjes, J. Francis, and Donald R. Knudson. *Recommendations for the Boston Globe Library*. (MIT Report ESL-R-509) Cambridge, MA: Massachussetts Institute of Technology, 1973.

724. Reintjes, J. Francis, and Richard S. Marcus. "Computer Aided Processing of the News." ANPA Research Institute R.I. Bulletin no. 993 (1969): 161-168; Proceedings of the AFIPS Spring Joint Computer Conference. New York, May 1969.

725. "Retrieval System Combines Computer and Microfiche." Editor and Publisher 107 (April 13, 1974): 33.

726. "Retrieval System Speeds Research." Editor and Publisher 109 (November 13, 1976): 50+.

727. Rhydwen, David A. "Computerized Storage and Retrieval of Newspaper Stories at the Globe and Mail Library, Toronto, Canada." Special Libraries 68 (February 1977): 57-61.

728. Rhydwen, David A. "Newspaper Library Automation Update (QL Systems)." Paper presented at the 68th Annual Conference of the Special Libraries Association, New York, NY, 5-9 June 1977. (ANPA 77-12)

729. Roblee, Martha. "New York Times Information Bank Provided Quick Easy Reference." Library Occurrent 26 (May 1978): 59-62.

730. Rosenfeld, Arnold. "New Technologies, New Frontiers." Paper presented at the 73rd Annual Conference of the Special Libraries Association, Detroit, MI, 5-10 June 1982. (ANPA 82-6)

731. Ross, Nina M. "Newspaper Databases." In National Online Meeting Proceedings - 1981, compiled by Martha E. Williams and Thomas H. Hogan, 415-420. Medford, NJ: Learned Information, Inc., 1981.

732. Ross, Nina M. "Newspaper Databases Update, 1982." In National Online Meeting Proceedings - 1983, compiled by Martha E. Williams and Thomas H. Hogan, 463-472. Medford, NJ: Learned Information, Inc., 1983.

733. Rothman, John. "Automated Information Processing at <u>The New York Times</u>." In <u>Proceedings of the American Society for Information Science, Annual Meeting</u>, vol. 5, 85-87. New York: Greenwood Publishing Corp., 1968.

734. Rothman, John. "The Electronic Newspaper -- Its Effect on the Newspaper Library." Paper presented at the 68th Annual Conference of the Special Libraries Association, New York, NY, 5-9 June 1977. (ANPA 77-13)

735. Rothman, John. "The New York Times Information Bank." <u>Special Libraries</u> 63 (March 1972): 111-115. Paper presented at the 62nd Annual Conference of the Special Libraries Association, San Francisco, CA, 6-10 June 1971. (ANPA 71-2)

736. Rothman, John. "The Times Information Bank on Campus." <u>Educom</u> 8 (Fall 1973): 14-19.

737. Russell, Beverly; Sharon Reeves; and Gail McLaughlin. "The Effects of Automation on Your Library Staff." Program presented at the 76th Annual Conference of the Special Libraries Association, Winnipeg, Canada, 8-13 June 1985.

738. Salton, G. "Automatic Processing of Current Affairs Queries." <u>Information Storage and Retrieval</u> 9 (March 1973): 165-180.

739. Sander, Linda K. "BASIS -- An Innovative Newspaper Library System." Paper presented at the 73rd Annual Conference of the Special Libraries Association, Detroit, MI 5-10 June 1982. (ANPA 82-2)

740. Sander, Linda K., and S.I. Richard. "Automating the Newspaper Library with BASIS." In <u>American Society for Information Science Proceedings</u>, v. 19, 262-264. White Plains, NY: Knowledge Industry Publications, Inc., 1982.

741. Schaeffer, Rex. "Computer Printed Control File: Phase II." Paper presented at the 60th Annual Conference of the Special Libraries Association, Montreal, Canada, 1-5 June 1969. (ANPA 69-10)

742. Schaeffer, Rex. "Punched Card Indexing for Newspaper Libraries." Paper presented at the 55th Annual Conference of the Special Libraries Association, St. Louis, MO, 7-11 June 1964. (ANPA 64-9)

743. Schill, Arthur C. "Bring the Morgue to Life (Managing Newspaper Information)." Paper presented at the 67th Annual Conference of the Special Libraries Association, Denver, CO, 6-10 June 1976. (ANPA 76-10)

744. Schmitz-Esser, W. "Review of the World's Press Information Banks." In *Second International Online Information Meeting*, London, 1978, 5-7 December 1978, 243-250. Oxford, England: Learned Information, 1979.

745. Schoenfeld, Alison. "Miracode for a Newspaper Library." Paper presented at the 63rd Annual Conference of the Special Libraries Association, Boston, MA, 4-8 June 1972. (ANPA 72-6)

746. Scofield, James S. "The Library." *Editor and Publisher* 100 (September 30, 1967): 7.

747. Slade, Ernest E. "Oakland Press Editorial Library System." Paper presented at the 74th Annual Conference of the Special Libraries Association, New Orleans, LA, 4-9 June 1983. (ANPA 83-4)

748. Smith, Stephen. "Online News Retrieval Systems Evaluations and Library Application." *Reference Services Review* 10 (Winter 1982): 47-60.

749. Stack, John P. "Computer Assisted Microform Retrieval at the *Daily Mirror*." *Reprographics Quarterly* 15 (Autumn 1982): 146-148.

750. Stelmicki, Russ. "Teletext in the Canadian Environment." Paper presented at the 70th Annual Conference of the Special Libraries Association, Honolulu, HI, 9-14 June 1979. (ANPA 79-6)

751. Stephens, Eileen. "Introduction to Computer Technology." Paper presented at the 72nd Annual Conference of the Special Libraries Association, Atlanta, GA, 13-18 June 1981. (ANPA 81-12)

752. Stephens, Eileen. "Systems Analysis." Paper presented at the 72nd Annual Conference of the Special Libraries Association, Atlanta, GA, 13-18 June 1981. (ANPA 81-13)

753. Stoddard, Nan W. "Unidas System." Paper presented at the 71st Annual Conference of the Special Libraries Association, Washington, DC, 7-12 June 1980. (ANPA 80-12)

754. Stoddard, Nan W. "Unidas System Replaces Morgue at St. Louis Post-Dispatch Library." Show-Me Libraries 35 (October - November 1983): 40-42.

755. Surace, Cecily J. "Newspaper Full Text Database Planning." Paper presented at the 75th Annual Conference of the Special Libraries Association, New York, NY, 9-14 June 1984. (ANPA 84-10)

756. Suratt, Samuel T. "Orientation Film Transcript." Paper presented at the 68th Annual Conference of the Special Libraries Association, New York, NY, 5-9 June 1977. (ANPA 77-14)

757. Szigethy, Marion. "A Computer Produced Thesaurus for the Clipping File." Paper presented at the 61st Annual Conference of the Special Libraries Association, Detroit, MI, 7-11 June 1970. (ANPA 70-6)

758. Tenopir, Carol. "Newspapers Online." Library Journal 109 (March 1, 1984): 452-453.

759. Tharp, Leonard. "Info-Ky: The Electronic Library That Shows You the Way It Really Is." Paper presented at the 71st Annual Conference of the Special Libraries Association, Washington, DC, 7-12 June 1980. (ANPA 80-13)

760. "Times Info Bank Hikes Prices." Library Journal 100 (May 15, 1975): 907.

761. "The Times Information Bank." *Wilson Library Bulletin* 43 (May 1969): 826.

762. Trimble, Kathleen. "Newspaper Libraries - Automated and Non-Automated Systems." *Editor and Publisher* 113 (January 12, 1980): 16-17.

763. Trivedi, Harish, and Barbara Newcombe. "The Story of a Neglected Resource: Information Storage and Retrieval in Newspaper Libraries." Paper presented at the First International Information Conference, Cairo, Egypt, 1982.

764. Unger, Harlow G. "Instant Data from the *New York Times*." *Canadian Business Magazine* 50 (October 1977): 13+.

765. "Use of Production Computers in Library Is Recommended." *Editor and Publisher* 107 (January 12, 1974): 27.

766. Vance, Julia M. "Trends in Newspaper Libraries." Paper presented at the 68th Annual Conference of the Special Libraries Association, New York, NY, 5-9 June 1977. (ANPA 77-15)

767. Voges, Mickie, and others. *Recommended Systems for the Incremental Automation of the Morgue of 'The Daily Texan'*. Arlington, VA: ERIC Document Reproduction Service, ED 146 932, June 1976.

768. Walker, Tom. "Computers Give New Life to Morgues." *Presstime* 4 (December 1982): 4-9.

769. Webber, Olga, and others. "Management of Auxiliary Storage and Retrieval Systems, Including Transcript of Discussion and Talks." Presented at the 59th Annual Conference of the Special Libraries Association, Los Angeles, CA, 2-7 June 1968. (ANPA 68-2)

770. Wedemeyer, Dan. "Teletext and the Role of the Information Provider - Entrepreneur?" Paper presented at the 70th Annual Conference of the Special Libraries Association, Honolulu, HI, 9-14 June 1979. (ANPA 79-7)

771. Werner, John R. "The Electronic Newspaper--Its Implications in the Newsroom." Paper presented at the 68th Annual Conference of the Special Libraries Association, New York, NY, 5-9 June 1977. (ANPA 77-16)

772. Whatmore, Geoffrey. "An Informal Commentary on Marion Szigethy's 'A Computer Produced Thesaurus for the Clipping File.'" Paper presented at the 61st Annual Conference of the Special Libraries Association, Detroit, MI, 7-11 June 1970. (ANPA 70-7)

773. Whatmore, Geoffrey. "News Libraries and the Future." In *Progessive Library Science*, edited by Robert L. Collison, 190-203. London: Butterworth, 1966.

774. Whatmore, Geoffrey; John Daligan; and Tony Archard. "A Microfilm System for Press Cuttings." *Reprographics Quarterly* 10 (April 1977): 49-51.

775. Whiteley, Jon. "Danish Database." *Systems International* 9 (May 1981): 53-54.

776. Wilken, Earl. W. "Information Centers -- Future Impact." *Editor and Publisher* 110 (April 30, 1977): 20, 78.

777. Wilken, Earl W. "Librarians State Concern Over System Designs." *Editor and Publisher* 110 (June 11, 1977): 89.

778. Wilken, Earl W. "Managing Editors and New Technology." *Editor and Publisher* 109 (November 13, 1976): 49.

779. Wilken, Earl W. "The Morgue Is Dead." *Editor and Publisher* (March 26, 1977): 16, 44-45.

780. Wilken, Earl W. "Should Newspapers Sell Stored Information?" *Editor and Publisher* 110 (August 13, 1977): 55.

781. Willmann, Donna. "First Look: VU/Text Databases."
     Online 9 (March 1985): 61-68.

782. Wood, Harry G. "Seminar Points Finger at Libraries'
     Service, Space." *Editor and Publisher* 104 (March 27, 1971):
     13-14.

NEWSPAPER LIBRARIANSHIP

783. "Alma Boynton Jacobus, 1893-1954." *Special Libraries* 45 (April 1954): 186.

784. Axford, William H. "New Dimensions for Newspaper Librarians." Paper presented at the 54th Annual Conference of the Special Libraries Association, Denver, CO, 9-13 June 1963. (ANPA 63-1)

785. Brown, Gerald D. "KSU (Kent State University) Course Directed to Library Decisions." *Editor and Publisher* 99 (February 12, 1966): 34.

786. Burness, Jack. "An Appeal to M.E.: Librarians Profit From Conventions." *Editor and Publisher* 95 (February 3, 1962): 62.

787. Craig, James C. "The Newspaper Librarian." *Special Libraries* 28 (September 1937): 247-249.

788. Davenport, Blanche J. "Survey of Newspaper Library Salaries." *Special Libraries Association Proceedings* 1 (1938): 79.

789. Hill, I. William. "Newspaper Librarians Blast Their Portrayal on Lou Grant." *Editor and Publisher* 113 (July 5, 1980): 28, 30.

790. "In Memory (Ralph J. Shoemaker)." *Kentucky Library Association Bulletin* 44 (Fall 1980): 20.

791. "Kentucky." *Southeastern Librarian* 28 (Winter 1978): 263. (Ralph J. Shoemaker chosen to first Newspaper Division roll of honor.)

792. Lewis, Chester Milton. "Transitions in Library Services, Newspaper Librarianship Today." *Special Libraries* 44 (November 1953): 363-365.

793. "Librarians Set Goal of Standards." *Editor and Publisher* 95 (July 7, 1962): 15, 54.

794. McCabe, Robert C. "The Newspaper Librarian." *Special Libraries* 35 (July-August 1944): 308-313. Paper presented at the 36th Annual Conference of the Special Libraries Association, Philadelphia, PA, 19-21 June 1944.

795. Macer-Wright, Sidney. "The Newspaper Librarian." In *Kemsley Manual of Journalism*, 275-280. London: Cassell and Company Limited, 1950.

796. "A Mass for Mae Nyquist Bowler Set for Monday at Sacred Heart." *New York Times*, 14 December 1979, sec. 4, p. 16.

797. Nelson, W.D. "Lou Grant's Librarian Under Fire." *Wilson Library Bulletin* 55 (September 1980): 47.

798. "Obituary." (David G. Rogers) *Special Libraries* 33 (March 1942): 101.

799. "Obituary - Ford M. Pettit." *Special Libraries* 43 (April 1952): 144.

800. "Obituary - William Alcott." *Special Libraries* 42 (February 1950): 68.

801. Orgain, Marian M. "Goals and Aims of Newspaper Libraries and Librarians." In *Special Librarianship: A New Reader, 1980*, edited by Eugene B. Jackson, 350-353. Metuchen, NJ: Scarecrow Press, 1980.

802. Santos, Helen S. "On Being a Newspaper Librarian." *ASLP Bulletin* 12 (June 1966): 33-34.

803. Sawyer, Agnes Looney. "A Preview of Newspaper Librarianship as a Profession; Field Is Uncrowded and Work Is Exciting." *Library Journal* 69 (April 15, 1944): 340-341.

804. "Special Library Profession and What It Offers: 1. Newspaper Libraries." Special Libraries 25 (September 1934): 189-195.

805. Vormelker, Rose L. "A Library School and a Course in Newspaper Librarianship." Paper presented at the 56th Annual Conference of the Special Libraries Association, Philadelphia, PA, 6-10 June 1965. (ANPA 65-14)

APPENDIX A: SOURCES OF ADDITIONAL INFORMATION

Two sources of information on newspaper libraries which no researcher should overlook are the Library of the American Newspaper Publishers Association and the Newspaper Division of the Special Libraries Association.

ANPA Library

The American Newspaper Publishers Association, founded in 1887, serves as a clearinghouse for member newspapers on all phases of the newspaper business. The ANPA Library houses an extensive collection of books, periodicals, documents and files on journalism, the newspaper business, mass communications, history, and selected titles in advertising and publishing. Highlights of the collection include works on newspaper layout and design, newspaper management, newsprint, press law, reporting and editing, the history of newspaper publishing, histories of newspapers, and biographies of newspaper publishers and other press figures.

In addition to serving as a reference source for information on the newspaper industry, the ANPA Library serves as a clearinghouse for information on newspaper libraries. Services offered by the Library include, but are not limited to, the following:

-- Transcripts of Newspaper Division speeches given at SLA's annual conferences since 1961 are on file in the library. References to these transcripts are listed in the bibliography with an ANPA reference number following the citation, e.g. ANPA 74-5. A complete list of the transcripts is available from the Library upon request.

-- Information packets covering various subjects of interest to newspaper librarians are available for loan. Subjects covered include newspaper library administration, automation, indexing, use of microforms, photo collections, manuals, reference collections, subject heading control, and filing rules. A complete list of packets with descriptions of each is available from the Library upon request.

-- The Library issues a newsletter, <u>Memorandum to Newspaper Librarians</u>, more commonly referred to as the "Library Memo." It contains news from the Newspaper Division of SLA, notes on books and articles of interest to newspaper librarians, notice of items available from the ANPA Library, order forms for transcripts of Newspaper Division speeches, and other news of interest to newspaper librarians. The newsletter is published at irregular intervals, one to three times a year.

For a description of the full range of services currently available from the ANPA Library, contact: ANPA Library, The Newspaper Center, Box 17407, Dulles International Airport, Washington, D.C. 20041.

Newspaper Division, SLA

The Newspaper Division of SLA, one of the organization's 32 divisions, was founded by Joseph F. Kwapil. Kwapil, of the Philadelphia Public Ledger, believed that "newspaper librarians could build better libraries if they could meet together." In 1923 Kwapil and a small group of newspaper librarians met at the Chelsea Hotel in Atlantic City for the first conference of the "Newspaper Group." Kwapil was appointed chairman of the committee on organization at the meeting. The following year the Newspaper Group officially affiliated with SLA.

Since that time the Newspaper Division has grown and prospered. Today workshops, seminars, meetings at SLA's annual conferences, and the Division members themselves provide perhaps the most important source of information available on newspaper libraries.

Pre-conference workshops at the annual meeting of SLA provide practical information on subjects covered, as well as give participants an opportunity to meet and talk with fellow newspaper librarians. The Division also sponsors regional workshops to meet the needs of librarians unable to attend the national meetings. Slide shows on several subjects (e.g. subject heading control, photo identification and preservation) are available for rental for a modest fee.

In 1974 the first edition of Guidelines for Newspaper Libraries was published by the American Newspaper Publishers Association Foundation. Written by members of the Newspaper Division, this manual contains "guidelines" for newspaper libraries on everything from "Starting the Library" to "Circulation Control" to "Newspaper Library Automation." Many chapters also include bibliographies of additional sources. The Guidelines, now in its second edition, is an invaluable source of information on newspaper libraries.

The newsletter of the Newspaper Division contains a wealth of information on newspaper libraries. First published in November of 1948 as the Bulletin of the Newspaper Group, the newsletter currently is published four times a year. News Library News contains reports of Division activities, articles on current trends and technology in newspaper libraries, announcements and reports on meetings of interest, personal items, plus much more. Members of the Newspaper Division receive the newsletter as part of their membership dues; non-member subscriptions are $20 a year.

Information on the Newspaper Division may be obtained by writing: Special Libraries Association, 1700 18th Street, N.W., Washington, D.C. 20009.

APPENDIX B: THESES, RESEARCH PAPERS ON NEWSPAPER LIBRARIES

Axelrod, Helene Bernice. "The History, Development, and Organization of the New York Times Library, and Contribution of the Times to Scholarship." Master's thesis, Southern Connecticut State College, 1965.

Breneau, Beth. "Local Press Indexing, A Personal Project." Reference Assistance Papers, No. 1. Wayne State University Libraries, July 1974.

Cohen, Diana M. "Content Analysis of Information about Newspapers and News Magazine Libraries in Selected Literature of Journalism, 1967-71." Research paper, Kent State University, 1973.

Colvin, Gloria Payne. "Bridging the Local Information Gap: A Proposal for Developing an Index to the Durham Morning Herald and the Durham Sun." Master's thesis, University of North Carolina, April 1980.

De'Ath, David. "A Survey of Newspaper Libraries and Their Problems." Master's thesis, City University (London), Centre for Information Science, 1977.

Galvin, Glenda I. "Index to Diamond Jubilee Issue of The Leader-Post." Master's thesis, Catholic University of America, May 1967.

Harris, Jeanette F. "The Newspaper Library: Its History, Function, and Value with Special Reference to the New York Herald Tribune." Master's thesis, Southern Connecticut State College, October 1959.

Lothrop, Jean W. "Indexing the Local Newspaper: An Economical Approach." South Dakota Library Bulletin 55 (October-December 1969): 227-236. (Subtitle: "Research paper presented to the Faculty of the Department of Librarianship, University of Denver, in Partial Fulfillment of the Requirements for the Degree of M.A.")

Mehta, D.S. "Newspaper Libraries." Master's thesis, Western Reserve University, School of Library Science, June 1955.

Mike, Sister Mary de Paul. "An Analytical, Cumulative Index to The Record (Louisville, KY) for the Years 1950 Through 1960." Master's thesis, Catholic University of America, 1966.

Nomer, Genevieve Trevor. "A Guide to Developing a Computerized Local News Index." Master's thesis, Glassboro State College, 1974.

Snowhite, Morton. "Techniques Used in Newspaper and Newspaper Libraries." Master's thesis, Drexel Institute of Technology, 1950.

Snyder, R. Seely. "The Newspaper Library in Philadelphia and Cleveland." Master's thesis, Western Reserve University, June 14, 1950.

Weems, Eddie J. "A Study of American Newspaper Libraries." Master's thesis, Florida State University, August 1954.

Williams, Charles R. "Role of the Newspaper Library." Master's thesis, University of Mississippi, June 1957.

Williamson, Wilbert E. "Indexes to Michigan Newspapers." Reference Assistance Papers No. 3. Wayne State University Libraries, March 1975.

Wolcoff, P. "Organization and Functioning of the New York Times Clipping Files." Master's thesis, Pratt Institute Library School, 1954.

APPENDIX C: PARTIAL LIST OF SLA CONFERENCES

1934	June 19-23	New York, NY	26th
1935	June 11-15	Boston, MA	27th
1936	June 16-19	Montreal, Canada	28th
1937	June 16-19	New York, NY	29th
1938	June 7-11	Pittsburgh, PA	30th
1939	May 23-27	Baltimore, MD	31st
1940	June 3-6	Indianapolis, IN	32nd
1941	June 16-19	Hartford, CT	33rd
1942	June 17-20	Detroit, MI	34th
1943	June 21-25	New York, NY	35th
1944	June 19-21	Philadelphia, PA	36th
1945	(None held because of World War II)		
1946	June 13-15	Boston, MA	37th
1947	June 10-13	Chicago, IL	38th
1948	June 6-11	Washington, DC	39th
1949	June 11-18	Los Angeles, CA	40th
1950	June 12-16	Atlanta City, NJ	41st
1951	June 18-21	St. Paul, MN	42nd
1952	May 26-29	New York, NY	43rd
1953	June 22-25	Toronto, Canada	44th
1954	May 17-22	Cincinnato, OH	45th
1955	June 12-17	Detroit, MI	46th
1956	June 3-7	Pittsburgh, PA	47th
1957	May 26-31	Boston, MA	48th

1958	June 8-12	Chicago, IL	49th
1959	May 31-June 4	Atlantic City, NJ	50th
1960	June 5-8	Cleveland, OH	51st
1961	May 28-June 1	San Francisco, CA	52nd
1962	May 27-31	Washington, DC	53rd
1963	June 9-13	Denver, CO	54th
1964	June 7-11	St. Louis, MO	55th
1965	June 6-10	Philadephia, PA	56th
1966	May 29-June 2	Minneapolis, MN	57th
1967	May 28-June 1	New York, NY	58th
1968	June 2-7	Los Angeles, CA	59th
1969	June 1-5	Montreal, Canada	60th
1970	June 7-11	Detroit, MI	61st
1971	June 6-10	San Francisco, CA	62nd
1972	June 4-8	Boston, MA	63rd
1973	June 10-14	Pittsburgh, PA	64th
1974	June 9-13	Toronto, Canada	65th
1975	June 8-12	Chicago, IL	66th
1976	June 6-10	Denver, CO	67th
1977	June 5-9	New York, NY	68th
1978	June 10-15	Kansas City, MO	69th
1979	June 9-14	Honolulu, HI	70th
1980	June 7-12	Washington, DC	71st
1981	June 13-18	Atlanta, GA	72nd
1982	June 5-10	Detroit, MI	73rd
1983	June 4-9	New Orleans, LA	74th

1984	June 9-14	New York, NY	75th
1985	June 8-13	Winnipeg, Canada	76th

AUTHOR INDEX

References below are to entry numbers, not to page numbers.

Abramson, Abe: 289

Ahnen, Paul: 567

Albert, W.J.: 2

Alcott, William: 3, 4

Altschull, Herbert: 5

Anderson, Elizabeth L.: 6

Andrews, Elliott E.: 239, 240

Arany, Lawrence A.: 7, 140

Archard, Tony: 563

Armstrong, Thomas F.: 404

Artman, Brenda: 442

Ashe, Reid: 570

Atkinson, Rose Marie: 390

Austin, Neal F.: 10

Axelrod, Helene Bernice: 142

Axford, William H.: 784

Bachelder, Sally: 574, 575

Baird, Kathleen Hunt: 576

Bant, Geoffery: 577

Barensfeld, Tom: 522, 578

Barger, Floyd: 11

Batliner, Doris: 580, 581

Bavakutty, M.: 294

Beegan, John F.: 295, 296

Bertleson, Arthur: 12

Betty, Samuel: 241

Billings, Thomas N.: 583

Birnbaum, Louis H.: 405

Bittinger, Betty Jo: 143

Blinn, Harold E.: 406

Bloom, Leon: 338

Borkowski, Casimir: 584

Brandenburg, George A.: 145

Breneau, Beth: 407

Breuer, M.H.: 297

Briscoe, Ellis: 298

Brown, Gerald D.: 785

Bruncken, Herbert: 408

Burell, Perry Jr.: 524

Burness, Jack K.: 13, 146, 147

Calixto-Aunario, Jesusa: 149

Cappiello, Alex: 588

Carrick, Kathleen: 14

Carter, J. Howard: 242

Castro, Leticia A.: 150

Catanese, Peter J.: 590

Cavanaugh, Bonnie: 412

Chao, Jennifer: 591, 592

Chapman, Ronald F.: 525

Chase, William D.: 15, 299, 318, 413

Cherry, Susan Spaeth: 414

Clark, Wesley C.: 151

Clemente-Carpio, Conchita: 152

Coates, Peter Ralph: 415

Cohen, Diana M.: 16

Cohen, Madeline: 17

Cole, Carol: 416

Collins, George M.: 594, 595

Colvin, Gloria Payne: 417

Conklin, Florina: 18, 302

Corcoran, Maureen: 597

Crabb, Margaret S.: 598

Crachi, Rocco: 153

Craig, James C.: 787

Criner, Kathleen: 599

Criswell, James: 303, 338

Curry, Arthur R.: 418

Curtiss, Frances E.: 154, 391

Cushman, Robert: 304

Dagg, Michael: 87

Daligan, John: 563

Daniel, Clifton: 19

Davenport. Blanche L.: 788

Davis, Bonnie M.: 601

Davis, Charles H.: 601

Dearnbarger, Dennis: 577

De'Ath, David: 20

Desmond, Robert W.: 21

Dewe, Michael: 419

Dezanni, David: 22

Dodge, John: 604

Doebler, Paul: 605

Doncevic, Lois A.: 526, 527

Drummond, Norman: 420

DuBois, Beatrice: 23

Duncan, E.E.: 609

Eads, Roscoe C.: 24, 25, 26, 27

Eaton, James J.: 421

Eggleston, Alma: 305

Einhorn, Judith Meister: 422

Ellis, Edgar: 29

Elston, Wilbur: 30

Epstein, Hank: 611

Everts, Helen: 296

Farquhar, Bob: 612, 613

Faulkner, Ronnie W.: 423

Faylona, Yolanda T.: 156

Feldmeir, Daryle: 157

Fenimore, Jean H.: 31

Fennell, Janice C.: 404

Ferguson, George V.: 159

Fikes, Robert Jr.: 424

Finberg, Howard: 306

Fingland, Geoffrey: 307

Fitch, Maude E.: 425

Foley, Kathy: 308

Fomerand, Raissa: 309

Forbes, Harold M.: 615

Foster, Paul P.: 160, 161, 426, 427

Fournier, Jacques: 530

Frankland, John: 310, 379, 428, 429, 517

Friedman, Harry A.: 430

Friendly, Alfred: 163

Furman, Sophia: 164

Furth, Stephen E.: 431

Galvin, Glenda I.: 432

Gardner, W. David: 619

Garoogian, Rhoda: 620

Garrison, Bruce: 621

Garthwaite, Joan: 33

Gephart, Joesph C.: 433

Ghosh, S.: 434

Gibbs-Smith, C.H.: 311

Gilzinger, Donald, Jr.: 435

Ginn, John C.: 34

Giovine, S. Richard: 165, 312

Gloede, Bill: 622

Goodman, Marian M.: 166

Gordon, David: 321

Goyal, Sat Paul: 436

Graham, Evarts A.: 243

Grayland, Eugene Charles: 35

Greene, Elwin S.: 244

Greene, Stephen A.: 36

Greengrass, Alan R.: 437, 623, 624

Griffin, John: 37

Griffin, Walter R.: 438

Gupte, Pranay: 39

Guzda, M.K.: 40

Gwinup, Thomas: 439

Hales, David A.: 440, 441, 442

Hall, George: 41

Hall, Sandy: 167, 245

Halloran, Vera: 42

Handy, Mary Jane: 626

Hannan, Mark: 318

Hansen, Inger: 87

Harr, Luther A.: 43

Harris, Jeanette F.: 44

Harris, Margaret: 443

Harris, Vivian: 314

Harrison, Alice W.: 315

Harrop, Mona: 444

Haswell, Martha Mullen: 532

Haughey, David: 628

Hayes, E. Kenneth: 629

Healey, Gerald B.: 630

Henebry, Agnes C.: 46, 47, 48, 168, 169, 316

Hermann, William H.: 534

Hill, I. William: 789

Hill, Joy: 317, 318

Hine, Gladys: 49

Hobby, Diana: 50

Hoffman, David M.: 51

Hogan, Thomas H.: 633

Holmes, Grace: 445

House, Audrey C.: 319

Hunt, Mary Alice: 52

Huskinson, A.H.: 53

Hutton, R.S.: 535

Inman, Robert P.: 170, 577

Ippolito, Andrew V.: 172, 638, 639, 536

Irwin, John: 449

Isaacs, Bob D.: 247, 248

Ivey, Robert: 320

Jackson, Miles M.: 640

Jacobus, Alma Boynton: 55, 173

James, Barbara: 450

Janda, Kenneth: 321

Jennings, Anne B.: 56, 452

Jessup, Lee Cheney: 57, 174

Johnpoll, Bernard K.: 453

Johnson, Dewayne B.: 58

Johnson, Josephine R.: 175, 249, 322, 392, 393

Jones, Nancy C.: 59

Jones, Robert W.: 60

Kabaker, Ray: 643

Kapecky, Michele Ann: 644, 645

Kearney, W. Robert: 601

Kehl, William B.: 646

Kesselman, Martin: 647

King, John: 323

King, Roy T.: 177, 538

Kirsh, Julie: 250, 251

Knee, Michael: 454, 455

Knudson, Donald R.: 649, 723

Koch, Jean E.: 456

Koenig, Michael E.D.: 252

Krayeski, Felix: 650

Kremer, Valerie: 61

Kruse, Rhoda: 457

Kumer, Mildred E.: 178

Kuzel, Judith F.: 458

Kyte, Colin H.J.: 459, 460

La Hood, Charles G., Jr.: 461

Ladenson, Alex: 462

Lage, Sondra B.: 651

Lal, Chhotey: 436

Lancaster, Frederick Wilfred: 652

Lathrop, Mary Lou: 253, 463

Lathrop, Norman M.: 463, 464

Lee, Leonard S.: 654

Legett, Anne: 324

Leigh-Bell, Peter: 655

Lewis, Chester Milton: 62, 179, 180, 181, 792

Lewis, Janice: 338

Lewis, Joseph: 63

Lindsay, Carol: 255, 256, 326

Long, John C.: 659

Lothrop, Jean W.: 465

Luecke, Camilla P.: 327

Luedtke, Kurt: 257

Lundy, Karen L.: 466

Lutz, Doug: 64

Lyon, Bill Jr.: 328

McArthur, D.W.: 539

McCabe, Robert C.: 794

McCardle, L.: 65

McCarthy, Joseph F.: 258, 318, 329

McCleary, Hunter: 661

McConnell, Robert: 662

McCormick, Robert R.:   193

McDermott, Philip Wayne: 467

McDonald, Lany W.:   330, 394

McGraw, Mary Drue: 66

Macer-Wright, Sidney: 795

Majumdar, Gopal Kumar: 540

McLaughlin, Gail: 275

Marble, Carol: 665

Marcus, Richard S.:   649, 651, 713, 724

Martin, Homer E. Jr.:   260, 261, 667, 668, 669

Martyn, Charles: 296

May, Barbara: 331

Mecinski, Harry R.:   328

Medley, Nora: 332

Mehta, D.S.:   67

Mest, Elizabeth: 674

Meyers, Pamela: 468

Michael, James J.:   469

Michaels, Andrea: 262

Michaels, David: 262

Mike, Sister Mary de Paul: 470

Miller, Diane: 68, 542

Miller, Tim: 676, 677, 678

Mills, T.F.:   471

Milner, Anita Cheek: 472

Milstead, Jessica L.:   473

Miniter, John J.: 263

Mischo, William H.: 474

Mohr, Euruce Collins: 69

Montague, P. McC.: 680

Mooney, Shirley E.: 70, 544

Moore, Waldo H.: 333

Nash, Mary M.: 684

Ndau, H.W.: 71

Nelson, W.D.: 797

Newcombe, Barbara: 306, 691, 763

Newman, John: 475

Nomer, Genevieve Trevor: 480

Noyes, Linwood I.: 76

Oetting, E.C.: 482

Oppedahl, Alison: 265, 338, 701

Orcutt, Helen M.: 339

Orgain, Marian M.: 77, 266, 267

Palmer, E. Clephan: 78

Parch, Grace D.: 5, 79

Parsley, Leslie: 268, 340, 379

Pasqua, Tom: 483

Pemberton, J.K.: 706

Perez, Ernest R.: 307, 341, 342, 707, 708, 709, 710

Perica, Esther: 484, 485

Perkins, Don: 269

Petersen, Agnes J.: 80, 270

Pettit, Ford M.: 81, 271, 343, 344

Philip, D.M.: 208

Ploch, Richard: 272

Polansky, Robert B.: 713

Power, Eugene B.: 345

Prensky, Milton: 13, 346

Prince, Vivian: 347

Provenzano, Domenic: 716

Quill, Edward: 487, 517

Quint, Barbara: 718

Radolf, Andrew: 719

Raines, Elaine Y.: 349

Rasmussen, Jay L.: 438

Ravenna, Lauretta: 395

Rawlinson, Alfred: 488

Raye, Sally: 489

Rayfield, Robert: 483

Redus, Mary Edith: 509

Reeves, Sharon: 275

Reinke, Mary: 490

Reintjes, J. Francis: 646, 721, 722, 723, 724

Reitman, Jo: 211

Rettig, James: 492

Rhydwen, David A.: 350, 351, 352, 353, 354, 355, 396, 397, 549, 551, 727, 728

Richard, S.I.: 740

Richards, Dargen A.:   273

Richstad, Jim: 37

Richter, Patricia: 475

Riker, Elaine M.:   356

Roberts, Linda: 489

Roblee, Martha: 729

Rogers, David G.:   553

Rosenfeld, Arnold: 730

Ross, Nina M.:   731, 732

Rothman, John: 733, 734, 735, 736

Rouse, J. Michael: 83

Rupp, Carla Marie: 213

Russell, Beverly: 275

Salton, G.:   738

Samyasam Mukhopadhyay: 84

Sander, Linda K.:   739, 740

Sandt, Roger W.:   555

Sanger, Chester W.:   215, 216, 357, 358

Santos, Helen S.:   802

Sardella, Mark: 217

Sausedo, Ann: 359, 496

Sawyer, Agnes Looney: 803

Schaeffer, Rex: 85, 86, 342, 360, 361, 362, 497, 741

Schill, Arthur C.:   743

Schmidt, Richard: 87, 556, 557

Schmitz-Esser, W.:   744

Schoenfeld, Alison: 530, 558

Scofield, James S.:   88, 89, 90, 91, 277, 306, 746

Scorza, Joseph C.:   416

Seeliger, Ronald: 499

Sell, Kenneth D.:   500

Semonche, Barbara P.:   93, 94, 278, 279, 501, 532

Shaftesley, John M.:   95, 502

Sharma, K.L.:   96, 280

Shoemaker, Ralph Joseph: 97, 98, 218, 219, 363, 364, 365

Sholtys, Pauline M.:   504

Shook, Sally: 449

Showalter, Stuart: 483

Simmons, Joseph M.:   99, 220, 221

Slade, Ernest E.:   747

Slate, Joseph Evans: 223

Slate, Ted: 100

Sloan, W.J.:   366

Slote, Stanley J.:   367

Smith, (Major General):   102

Smith, Donald R.:   505

Smith, Evelyn E.:   101, 399

Smith, Stephen: 748

Smutny, Charles T.:   224

Smythe, Eric J.C.:   103, 368

Snowhite, Morton: 104

Snyder, R. Seely: 105

Somers, Lewis S.: 369

Soosai, J.S.: 37

Spriers, David: 559

Stack, John P.: 560

Stafford, Robert: 506

Stelmicki, Russ: 750

Stephens, Eileen: 751, 752

Stern, Joan: 370

Stevens, Robert: 107

Stewart, James D.: 75

Stewart, Robert W.: 507

Stoddard, Nancy: 753, 754

Stolberg, Charles: 226

Stout, Ruth: 371

Sullivan, Bernice: 108, 374

Surace, Cecily J.: 228, 755

Suratt, Samuel T.: 756

Suvak, Daniel: 508

Sykes, Cyril: 109

Symonds, Maurice: 375, 376

Szigethy, Marion: 377

Tashima, Takumi: 525

Tauber, Alfred S.: 511

Tenopir, Carol: 758

Tharp, Leonard: 759

Thaxton, Lyn: 509

Thomas, Alfred: 229

Thomas, Lou: 230, 281, 282, 307

Thompson, Gayle: 379

Thorogood, Horace: 112

Tiffen, James F.: 283

Tiffen, Pauline: 283

Tomlinson, Laurence E.: 510

Trice, Tom: 512

Trimble, Kathleen: 113, 284, 400, 762

Trivedi, Harish: 380, 691, 763

Tucker, D.S.: 114

Unger, Harlow G.: 764

Vance, Julia M.: 561, 766

Ver Hulz, Jack: 511

Vierra, Bobbie: 512

Visconty, Jean: 116

Viskochil, Larry A.: 381

Vitek, Clement G.: 13, 382, 513, 514

Voges, Mickie: 767

Varmelker, Rose L.: 117, 805

Walker, Joy M.: 118, 342

Walker, Marie-Anne E.: 515

Walker, Tom: 768

Wallis, Elizabeth J.: 516

Webber, Olga: 383, 517

Wedemeyer, Dan: 770

Weems, Eddie J.: 119, 120, 121

Weiller, Herman E.: 122

Welch, Mary: 123

Wells, Chris: 286

Werner, John R.: 771

Whatmore, Geoffrey: 124, 125, 126, 127, 128, 129, 130, 232, 233, 384, 563, 772, 773

Whiteley, Jon: 775

Whitworth, Bess: 131, 132

Wilken, Earl W.: 776, 777, 778, 779, 780

Williams, Charles R.: 133

Williamson, Wilbert E.: 519

Willmann, Donna: 781

Winchell, F. Mabel: 520

Wixom, Sharon Elizabeth-Lee S.: 287

Wolcoff, P.: 235

Wolf, David: 385

Wood, Ellen: 288, 386, 401

Wood, Harry G.: 135

Woodhouse, Renie: 236

Wright, Palmer H.: 136

Wright, Walter: 137

Yingling, John: 388

Zarcone, Beth B.: 389

Zeskey, Russell H.: 521

Zimmerman, Peter J.: 138

Zweifel, Dick: 87

SUBJECT INDEX

References below are to entry numbers, not to page numbers.

ABC News Information Center: 17

ANPA

   SEE: American Newspaper Publishers Association

ACCESS: 338

Akron (OH) Beacon Journal: 290

Alcott, William: 800

American Newspaper Publishers Association: 1, 23, 102, 110, 259, 523, 564, 565, 646, 777

American Press Institute: 73, 111, 657

ANCIRS: 293, 338, 560, 669, 725

Annon, Ruth: 213

Archives: 8, 99, 171

Arizona Champion-Coconino Sun: 449

Arkansas Gazette (Little Rock, AR): 143, 229

Atex: 586, 703, 715

Atlanta (GA) Constitution: 509, 603

Atlanta (GA) Journal: 603

Atlantic City (NJ) Press: 480

Australia: 506

Awards: 162, 163

BASIS: 582, 612, 622, 669, 700, 739, 740

BASIL: 655

Beacon Journal (Akron, OH): 446, 476

Bell and Howell: 468, 554

Binding: 55

Book Reviews: 5, 51

Boston (MA) Globe: 123, 144, 217, 585, 586, 591, 594, 604, 714, 723, 744, 765

Boston (MA) Herald: 297

Boston (MA) Traveler: 297

Bowler, Mae Nyquist: 796

Braun, Ruth: 189

Broadcast News Media Libraries: 17, 64

BRS/Search: 669

Budgets: 248, 252, 256, 265, 266

Bulletins: 181

Bureau of Advertising: 42

Burness, Jack K.: 163, 188

Call-Chronicle Newspaper (Allentown, PA): 674

Canadian News Index: 409, 410, 453

Cape Argus: 415

Chase, William D.: 115, 657

Chicago (IL) American: 59

Chicago (IL) Daily News: 59, 99, 220, 221

Chicago (IL) Journal of Commerce: 164

Chicago (IL) Sun-Times: 59, 99, 220, 221, 726

Chicago (IL) Today: 254

Chicago (IL) Tribune: 59, 193, 224, 254

Christian Science Monitor: 215, 357

Christian Science Publishing Society: 300

Cleveland (OH) News: 105

Cleveland (OH) Plain Dealer: 105

Cleveland (OH) Press: 105, 522

Collins, George C.:   217

Columbia University: 134

Commercial Databases: 394, 638

Compact Disks: 678

Computer Terminology: 644, 645

Congressional Research Service: 571, 650

CONTEXT: 566

Conventions: 146

Copyright: 333, 386

Courier-Journal (Louisville, KY):   175, 659, 744

Daily Illini: 577

Daily Oklahoman (Oklahoma City, OK):   74, 600, 612, 613

Daily Pantagraph (Bloomington, IL):   68, 542

The Daily Texan (Austin, TX):   767

The Dallas (TX) Morning News: 331

DATATEK: 678

Dayton (OH) Daily News: 492

Decatur (IL) Herald-Review: 168, 169

Des Moines (IA) Register: 474

Detroit (MI) Free Press: 530, 567

Detroit (MI) News: 154, 178, 271, 343, 530

Directories: 5, 6, 79

Directory of Newspaper Libraries in the U.S. and Canada: 5, 79

DOCU/Master: 603, 669, 775

Docherty, Pearl A.: 140

Doohan, John: 184, 528

Durham (NC) Morning Herald: 417, 501, 532

Durham (NC) Sun: 417, 501, 532

Eads, Roscoe: 141

Electronic Library System: 587, 669

Elizabeth (NJ) Daily Journal: 507

Equipment: 286

F.B.I.: 3

Flint (MI) Journal: 115, 464, 480

Flint (MI) Journal Project: 413, 464

Foreign Names: 358

Frankland, John: 184

Freedom of Information: 87

Full Text Systems: 611, 709, 755

The Globe and Mail (Toronto, Canada): 350, 352, 353, 684, 692, 727, 731, 744

Globedata: 585

Government Documents: 390, 400

Grand Forks (ND) Herald: 455

Grant, Lou: 789, 797

Graphics: 306

Greensboro (NC) Daily News: 498

Greensboro (NC) Record: 498

The Guardian (London, England): 625

Guidelines for Newspaper Libraries: 38, 259

The Hackensack (NJ) Record: 480

Henebry, Agnes C.: 139

Herbert vs. Lando: 22, 288

History: 140, 160

Holograms: 627

Honolulu (HI) Star Bulletin: 525

Houston (TX) Chronicle: 267

Image Systems, Inc.: 293, 725

India: 436

Indianapolis (IN) News: 140

Indianapolis (IN) Star: 140

Info Globe: 692

Info-KY News Retrieval System: 658, 659, 694, 759

Information Bureaus: 29, 62

Infotex Inc.: 622, 669, 703

Inquire/Text: 669

Insurance: 54

INTREX: 564

Ippolito, Andrew V.: 184

Jacobus, Alma Boynton: 783

Jennings, Anne B.: 162

Jersey (Jersey City, NJ) Journal: 507

Jessup, Lee Cheney: 182

Jewish Chronicle: 502

Johnpoll, Bernard K.: 410

Johnson, Josephine R.: 162, 184

Journal-American: 223

Journal Herald (Dayton, OH): 380

Kalamazoo (MI) Gazette: 466

Kalvar: 353, 354

Kansas City (MO) Star: 528

Kent State University: 785

Knight-Ridder: 648, 677, 719

Kwapil, Joseph F.: 160

Lasers: 627

Lathrop, Mary Lou: 414

Lathrop, Norman: 414

Leader-Post (Saskatchewan): 432

Lektrievers: 196, 573, 598, 746

Letters: 575

Lewis, Chester Milton: 182, 189

Libel: 21, 242, 288

Library Manuals: 4, 225, 239, 240, 259, 268, 287, 290, 295, 340, 358, 359, 360, 371, 374

Library Schools: 565, 805

Life: 305

Lincoln (NE) Journal-Star: 374

Lockheed Information Systems: 568

London Gazette: 445

Los Angeles (CA) Times: 8, 228, 301, 744

Louisville (KY) Times: 175, 659, 744

M.I.T.

   SEE: Massachusettes Institute of Technology

Manchester Guardian: 233

Manila Chronicle: 152

Manila Daily Bulletin: 149

Manila Times: 150

Manual for Newspaper Library: 4

Massachusettes Institute of Technology (MIT): 564, 646, 651, 724, 723, 765

Maughan, Charles: 140

Mead Systems: 590, 595, 597, 633, 671, 672, 687, 692, 698, 704, 706, 707, 714, 716, 731

Medill School of Journalism: 321

Micrographic System: 654

Milwaukee (WI) Journal: 211, 379, 429

Milwaukee (WI) Sentinel: 211, 379, 408

MIRACODE: 321, 338, 530, 558

Mirror Group Newspapers: 560

Montreal-Star: 225

Moore, Charles T.: 140

Morgue Directory System: 777

Morning Advocate: 230

Mycro-Tek: 577

Nashville (TN) Banner: 174, 489

The National Enquirer (Lantana, FL): 213

National Online Meeting: 731, 732

New York Herald Tribune: 44, 197, 207, 237

New York Journal-American: 45, 190

New York News: 196

New York Times: 39, 142, 179, 191, 210, 235, 334, 366, 388, 714, 744

New York Times Information Bank: 334, 433, 437, 571, 574, 575, 585, 597, 605, 609, 614, 619, 620, 623, 624, 634, 635, 636, 647, 664, 671, 687, 688, 689, 690, 697, 706, 712, 729, 733, 735, 736, 760, 761, 764

New York Times Thesaurus of Descriptors: 334, 378

New York World Telegram and Sun: 195, 207, 237

Newark (NJ) Evening News: 72

Newark Public Library: 72

Newark (NJ) Star Ledger: 480

News Databases: 661, 662, 672, 676, 677, 685, 686, 691, 692, 716, 718, 719, 731, 732, 748, 758, 781 (See Also: New York Times Information Bank)

News Meadia: 707

Newsday (LI): 435, 573, 598, 746

Newspaper Digest: 405

Newspaper Indexing Center: 447, 477, 521

Newspaper Libraries in the U.S. & Canada: 6

Newspaper Library Basics Seminar: 90, 255, 261, 299, 317, 326, 341, 766

Newstex: 685, 692

NEXIS: 698, 716, 731

Noland, Stephen C.: 140

Oakland Press (Pontiac, MI): 587, 596, 622, 747

Obituaries: 783, 798, 799, 800

Oklahoma City (OK) Times: 74, 600, 612, 613

Oppedahl, Alison: 162

Ottawa (Canada) Journal: 61

Ottawa (IL) Republican-Times: 136

Owensboro (KY) Messenger-Inquirer: 658

PDP 11/34: 703

PM (NY): 165

Palmer's Index to the Times: 450, 459, 460, 516

Pence, Harry: 198

Personnel: 241, 243, 244, 245, 247, 249, 251, 256, 270, 278, 279, 283, 737

Petersen, Agnes J.: 198

Pettit, Ford M.: 799

Philadelphia (PA) Daily News: 105, 704

Philadelphia (PA) Evening Bulletin: 105

Philadelphia (PA) Inquirer: 105, 160, 161, 704

Philippines Herald: 156

Photographs: 207, 237, 297, 299, 303, 304, 305, 306, 310, 311, 316, 317, 318, 319, 327, 328, 329, 333, 337, 343, 346, 351, 352, 353, 364, 367, 369, 370, 374, 375, 376, 381, 386, 388, 389

Politiken (Copenhagen, Denmark): 775

Providence (RI) Journal News: 239

Public Access: 88, 258, 277, 307

Putnam, Mac E.: 140

Q.L. Systems: 567, 669, 685, 692, 707, 728

Ragen MRS-90: 588, 682

The Record (Hackensack, NJ): 507

The Record (Louisville, KY): 470

Redding, Matthew: 198

Reporters: 137, 652

Research: 212

Rogers, David G.: 798

Rothman, John: 191, 334

St. Louis (MO) Post-Dispatch: 177, 243, 538, 754

St. Louis Public Library: 469

St. Paul (MN) Dispatch: 480

St. Paul (MN) Pioneer Press: 480

St. Petersburg (FL) Evening Independent: 234

St. Petersburg (FL) Times: 234

Salaries: 788

San Diego (CA) Herald: 425, 457

San Diego (CA) Union: 425, 457, 494

San Francisco (CA) Chronicle: 166

San Francisco (CA) Examiner: 166, 335, 554

San Francisco (CA) News-Call-Bulletin: 166

Schaeffer, Rex: 325

Schramm, Alice M.: 139

Science Information Services: 116

Scottish Daily Record: 232

Scofield, James S.: 184, 656

Seattle (WA) Times: 18

Shoemaker, Ralph Joseph: 176, 790

SIRE: 669

SMART: 738

South African Library: 415

Southern National Canadian Database: 662

Southern Newspaper Publishers Association: 135

Southern Recorder (Milledgeville, GA): 404

Space Planning: 262

Special Libraries Association. Newspaper Division: 13, 82, 139, 141, 145, 146, 155, 158, 163, 167, 172, 180, 181, 182, 183, 184, 185, 186, 187, 188, 189, 192, 198, 199, 200, 201, 202, 203, 204, 205, 206, 212, 216, 218, 219, 226, 227, 231, 242, 695, 793, 804

STAIRS: 726

Standard and Mail: 415

Standards: 13, 82, 117, 183, 214, 216, 793

The Star (Johannesburg, South Africa): 208, 236

State Times: 230

STATUS: 669

Subject Headings: 203, 227, 239, 289, 290, 295, 298, 302, 312, 320, 322, 324, 326, 332, 339, 341, 342, 347, 349, 355, 357, 359, 361, 362, 377, 380, 382, 504, 772

Subpoenas: 254

Surveys: 1, 10, 26, 52, 228, 286, 394, 804

Symonds, Maurice: 198

Tax Deductions: 335

Teletext: 699, 750, 770

The Tennessean (Nashville, TN): 57, 489, 490

TEQLIB: 669

The Texas Observer (Austin, TX): 499

Text Enhancement: 709

Theses, Research Papers, etc.: 16, 20, 44, 67, 104, 105, 120, 121, 133, 142, 235, 407, 417, 432, 465, 470, 480, 519

Time Magazine: 173, 389, 738

The Times (London): 171, 450, 459, 460, 516

Times of India: 96

The Trenton Times: 367

UNIDAS: 669, 707, 753, 754

United Kingdom Papers: 20

U.S. News and World Report: 390, 400

U.S. Newspaper Project: 615, 683

UNIVAC: 454, 707

University of Texas: 45

Vancouver Sun: 598, 746

Viet Nam Press: 115

Vormelker, Rose: 785

VU/Text: 661, 676, 677, 692, 719, 781

WPA Projects: 405, 406, 408, 425, 462, 467, 478, 479, 486, 518, 534

<u>Wall Street Journal</u>:　555

War:　173, 312, 344, 376, 391

<u>Washington (DC) Post</u>:　147, 188, 473

Weeding:　285, 365, 367, 371, 383

<u>White Hall Register</u>:　518

Williams, Talcott:　134

Workshops:　32, 56, 90, 92, 101, 106, 135, 255, 264, 317, 766

<u>World-Journal-Tribune</u> (New York City):　337

World Reporter:　625

XM Retrieval System:　581

<u>Yorkshire Post</u>:　421

Zinc:　369

Zytron Data Systems:　629